KARMA ALIGNMENT NUMEROLOGY

DR. ROHET SETHI

BLUEROSE PUBLISHERS
India | U.K.

Copyright © Dr Rohet Sethi 2024

All rights reserved by author. No part of this publication may be reproduced, stored in a retrieval system, or transmitted in any form or by any means, electronic, mechanical, photocopying, recording or otherwise, without the prior permission of the author. Although every precaution has been taken to verify the accuracy of the information contained herein, the publisher assumes no responsibility for any errors or omissions. No liability is assumed for damages that may result from the use of information contained within.

BlueRose Publishers takes no responsibility for any damages, losses, or liabilities that may arise from the use or misuse of the information, products, or services provided in this publication.

For permissions requests or inquiries regarding this publication,
please contact:

BLUEROSE PUBLISHERS
www.BlueRoseONE.com
info@bluerosepublishers.com
+91 8882 898 898
+4407342408967

ISBN: 978-93-6452-666-1

Cover design: Shivani
Typesetting: Sagar

First Edition: October 2024

गुरू ब्रह्मा गुरू विष्णु, गुरु देवो महेश्वरा
गुरु साक्षात परब्रह्मा, तस्मै श्री गुरुवे नमः

Gurur Brahma Gurur Vishnu
Gurur Devo Mahesh Varah
Guru Shakshat Para Brahma
Tasmai Shri Guruve Namah

With eternal gratitude I dedicate this book to my parents, my best-half and to all my readers and followers who believe in the law of karma.

Acknowledgments

To begin with, I would like to pay my deepest gratitude to my editor Kanika Chopra Sehgal, who has been my ardent supporter and colleague throughout the journey of writing the book. Thanks to her enthusiasm and expertise, I was able to finish this book within the stipulated time-frame. With her unwavering determination and positivity, this book has been turned into a reality. Her feedback on the narrative was absolutely flawless.

To the entire team at Blue Rose Publications, my continued approbation for your fervour and competence in making this book a thing of beauty and a joy forever.

My deepest gratitude to my family, especially to my parents whose affection has been the foundation block of my career. Had not it been for my parents' support, I would have not entered this line of profession. And to my wife, for whom this book has been a surprise. Her unfathomable love encourages me to step forward in life. Her endless belief in me makes me stronger and courageous.

Finally, to YOU! Dear reader, I am indebted to you for keeping your faith, for stepping into the world of infinite possibilities with Karmic Alignment Numerology. There is an invisible power that has aligned your stars to read this grand revelation.

Prologue

यस्तविन्द्रियाणि मनसा नियम्यारभतेऽर्जुन |
कर्मेन्द्रियैः कर्मयोगमसक्तः स विशिष्यते || 7||

Yas tvindriyāṇi manasā niyamyārabhate 'rjuna
Karmendriyaiḥ karma-yogam asaktaḥ sa viśiṣhyate

When we try to control our senses through our mind with full determination, we are able to begin the karma yoga, which is carrying out the duties religiously while being detached from the fruits of the actions, only then we can perform to the best of our abilities.

Bhagavad Gita: Chapter 3, Verse 7

Karma is inevitable. We bear the consequences of our karma day in day out without a speck of thought that what if we already know what kind of karma we shall have to deal with in the next week or month. But imagine if something helps you to know what your future holds. What if you can control the course of your life? What if you get acquainted with the greater purpose of your life? What if you know how to heal yourselves?

So many what ifs, isn't it? On a scale of 10, how much do you want to know about your future or to deal with your present? In this contemporary epoch, life has become a virtual race wherein everyone is yearning for things uncountable infinitely however nobody is ready to understand the pertinence of leading a blissful life devoid of stress and contemplation. Hence unintentionally, each one of us keeps on performing karma which can rather hurt spiritually in this life or the next ones, thus escalating the karmic debt for the future. And whether one likes it or not, karma believes in the law that every action has an equal and opposite reaction, be it good or bad.

To mitigate with the most horrendous problem since the past centuries, a methodology named Karmic Numerology has been unearthed. This methodology is based on 22 karmic alignment numbers which are directly related to the major arcana cards of the tarot cards deck. The images are evident as per the interpretation of the cards. Every karma number is directly associated with the karmic lessons everyone has to undergo during their lifetime. A life star matrix is the formula which exhibits the exact karma numbers in the life of the inherent. Not every karmic alignment number can be found in a person's life star matrix owing to the fact that they must have dealt with certain karmas in the past incarnations and are left with the ones being exhibited. Hence those which are being seen have their own sets of tasks which have to be accomplished by the inherent in the stipulated time in order to free himself off of the karma.

These karmic alignment numbers are divided into four parts:

1. Karmic numbers 1-7: materialistic group

2. Karmic numbers 8-14: soul group

3. Karmic numbers 15-21: spiritual group

4. Karmic number 22: transitional group which connects the spiritual group with the materialistic.

The life star matrix is solely based on the date of the birth of the inherent hence the numbers play an indomitable part. Every karmic number has challenges to be dealt with and tests to be taken. If one is unable to pass the life tests, then the karmas shall keep on repeating over and over until the inherent passes them.

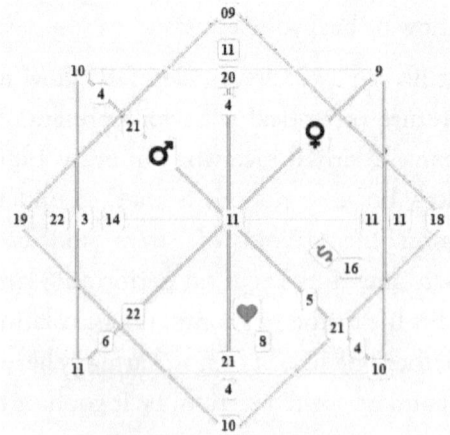

Since only the date of birth is the basis of the life star matrix, the next question which must have cropped up in your mind is that thousands of people have the same birth date then why do their personalities differ. The reason behind is as follows: the people work according to their karma. If one is aligning with the universe, there is no doubt about the fact that they will be able to spend their karma in a good way, beneficial for the greater good otherwise things can always go haywire.

There is another philosophy somewhat related to this theory which says that there are old souls and young souls. The older souls are the ones who had lived their life to the fullest in the past incarnation however due to their karmas, they had to take birth again. The younger souls are the ones who were bereft of living their life as much a human generally lives up to hence they died quite young in their last birth so again they had to take a birth to finish the tasks they were supposed to perform in the last birth. The older souls are mature, they have an understanding of how things work and how karmas have to be obliterated. It is up to them to decide whether they want to perform the good karma or the bad one. It is solely their responsibility however on the other side, the younger souls are the ones who hardly have any idea of how the karmas work for a long time. By the time they comprehend the philosophy of karma, they are already knee-deep in the quicksand by performing the karmas they never intended to if they had known the karma philosophy.

There are three types of karmas. The first and foremost is the karma in the present. We already know what we are doing hence we know what we are generating for the karma consequences-whether good or bad. The second one is the karma in the past. We hardly have any idea of what we did in the past incarnation hence there is no way of controlling the karmas but rather go with the flow of the life star matrix. The third type of karma is the karma we choose. Once we know that an action is spiritually wrong and can damage us and others too, even then if we wish to choose that karma over the good karma then it is the karma we choose to perform but we must not forget that karma does not need an address to reach us. Hence every task that we undertake is a karma, every thought we come across is a karma and every act we perform becomes a karma. We must become aware of how we are leading our lives for at the end of the day, only we have to bear the repercussions of our karmas.

This book focuses on what the karmic alignment numbers are, how do they work in the practical life, and how can one locate them in their life star matrix and understand their meanings through the help of the life star matric calculator. These numbers show the massive impact on the life of the inherent, his personality and his behaviour over a time period indicated through the matrix. As a matter of fact, one can read if he is going through the positive manifestation of a karmic alignment number or a negative one through the help of this book.

By the words positive manifestation, the book explores the behaviour which is generally considered good in a person. One can become benevolent while staying in touch with his inner self too. The life becomes smooth during the positive manifestation of the karma number however during the negative manifestation, the inherent can become quite the opposite of what he was in his positive manifestation such as if one was found benevolent as his positive characteristic, then during the negative one the tables turn and the person may become a stingy Scrooge. Negative characteristics invite troubles in the life of the inherent.

The behaviour can change the whole outlook of a person lest the future. Even the present feels heavy during the negative manifestation of the karmic alignment numbers. Through the help of the karmic alignment, one can transform his life into a beautiful fantasy. The karmic alignment shows that how one can change his approach while dealing with certain matters. When the inherent gets cognizant of how bad his behaviour is only then he can allow his subconscious mind to enter into the aligned form. His acknowledgement plays a vital role in transforming his life.

This methodology can be used to understand how karma works in everyone's life. While getting acquainted with the karmic alignment numbers, you can demystify the dark secrets of the world beyond our grasp. You can learn this art to know what kind of karmas you are yet to face, work accordingly and achieve what you have been aiming for.

The karmic alignment numbers are the way to tap into the future while attuning yourself with the universe. With every karma number, the karmic alignment is given so that you can comprehend the ways in which your life can take a turn for the best. The karmic alignment explains the steps towards the transformation. To get acquainted with the calculator, scan this QR Code.

Every karma number is explained with an introductory part which shows how and what the karma is about, in other words, the visual representation of the karma in words followed by positive characteristics and negative characteristics. To guide the reader in overcoming the obstacles, a detailed karmic alignment plan is discussed with every karmic alignment number. Finally an affirmation to deal with the peace-threatening issues which can be easily memorised by heart to forge the path of spiritual enlightenment. So without further ado, dive deep into this ocean of knowledge and unleash the potential which you thought you never had, unearth the secrets of your life which could have been left unheeded have you not made the right decision to buy this book. Because...

Karmic Alignment Numbers are the next best discovery after bread. It shall become as indispensable as water in the coming days in your life, you shall notice. And if the book-reading the book brings you to a crossroad in life of choosing the best of best, visit the site **https://rohetsethi.com.**

All the best for treading a secret path towards divinity and penultimate success.

Contents

1 The Magician 1
2 The High Priestess 11
3 The Empress 21
4 The Emperor 31
5 The Hierophant 43
6 The Lovers 53
7 The Chariot 63
8 Strength 73
9 The Hermit 81
10 The Wheel of Fortune 91
11 Justice 99
12 The Hanged Man 109
13 Death 119
14 Temperance 129
15 The Devil 137
16 The Tower 145
17 The Star 153
18 The Moon 161
19 The Sun 171
20 Judgement 179
21 The World 187
22 The Fool 193

1
THE MAGICIAN

Introduction

The master of manifestation, the 1st Karmic Alignment number THE MAGICIAN, is the symbol for resourcefulness, creativity, and self-empowerment with the infinite power of transformation. As the hermetic axiom goes, AS ABOVE SO BELOW, it deals with an unlimited potential exhibited by the sign of infinity.

'As above so below' can be interpreted as the spiritual and the material realms. The juggler puts his heart and soul in bridging the gap between the heaven and earth while tapping into the inner resources, and aligning the thoughts and actions with the highest potential. If there are negligible chances of a task, the miracle worker ensures that the universe move mountains to let the inherent achieve his goals.

The harnessing of power is done solely by the magician aka juggler. The presence of the magician's tools namely a wand, a pentacle, a sword and a cup symbolise the presence and amalgamation of earth, water, air and fire respectively to transform the ideas or the vision of the inherent into reality.

In the astrological context, The Magician is directly related to the planet Mercury thus if the energies of both are transfused, the inherent gets the ability to follow 'Saam Daam Dand Bhed' easily translated to English as the carrot and stick method, a method encapsulating either persuasion or coercion.

Positive Characteristics

The person under the 1st Karmic Alignment number is prone to extraordinary abilities solely dedicated to the divinity. If you fall under this category of karmic number, you must consider yourself as an innovator. You are someone who pioneers in fields unknown and are bestowed with abilities to catch the fireflies on a sunny day.

Due to the powers vested in you from divine channels, you are always confident about everything that you do. Owing to which you carry your divine aura everywhere thus dispelling darkness and doubts even for others. You are the light-bearer, an apostle of knowledge unknown.

With boundless happiness, you can move mountains for own benefits however you tend to keep multiple screening tests for others who want to get a glimpse of your ethereal world. Now for some, this might be an act of selfishness but for you, it is impertinent to protect your divine energies so that their after-results remain unknown to anyone and everyone. You firmly believe that divinity is only for those who are very well-aware of how it works in miraculous ways. And for those who have no idea what kind of incredible powers does divinity hold or the way it works, the magician in you decides for them whether they are allowed to take a peep in your mental premises or not.

With this particular karmic number in your matrix you must know that you are chosen for a reason. You are a satiable soul with high mental abilities but somehow for reasons unknown have fallen from grace. Leaving the reason and its repercussions for the negative manifestation of your character, your cognitive potential determines the communication.

According to your ways of the world, you prefer talking to the experts instead of the ones who are still walking towards the destination of expertise. You deem every moment as precious and as per your disposition, it must be utilised only when a sense of productivity can be registered afterwards. You have no place for trials in your pretty intense life. Although there is no harm in joining others in jibe however you tag along only with those who have a class or a level of authority. Your individuality puts gigantic emphasis on the eloquence, manner of style and clothing along with etiquette.

Since you belong to a divine power, directly channelling energies from the spiritual realm, you pick up vibes in a fraction of a second. You light up the dark rooms with your intelligence. You ensure that you bridge the gap between heaven and earth to manifest what you desire and want.

Undeniably, you love to be the cynosure, yet you share your ideas only with the ones who have authority and can approbate your knowledge and intellect. Nevertheless, you despise if anybody controls you or tries to be authoritative over you which tends to happen a lot and when it does, you are surely to cut off your ties with that person as you like to exercise control and it ticks off a nerve when you are controlled. Perplexing others, you route your way through this with making much of an effort.

Absolutely optimistic, the thrill in your blood is contagious. While you are a traveller by heart but there is still a chance that you have not yet discovered that you have an innate talent for being an explorer so leave the contemplating nature behind for a while when you can and give exploration a shot. You might carve a career for yourself out of it. Jack of all trades, you happen to the life of any party you go to. People crave for your presence owing to the amazing experiences of your life. Be it a failure (which seldom takes place) or a series of success- you are an inspiration for many.

No matter how old you are, you shall always feel like a teenage in his bloom. Being attuned with the higher energies, you radiate and shine like the sun.

Negative Characteristics

When somebody calls you a pioneer, how do you reckon that feel? Exalted? On the top of the world? It feels quite natural to feel powerful and to be able to control everything and everyone with each step towards success, doesn't it? However you must understand the fact that uneasy lies the head that wears the crown. With great power comes great responsibility. Behaving otherwise can practically take only hours to destroy what you had worked on for years in the past.

There is no doubt about the fact that you are a magician, metaphorically. You work hard, no doubt about it, but it is the divinity which rewards you for your hard work. The higher powers makes you who you are, not your deeds in the present birth.

Generally what happens is that you count yourself accountable for the success in life instead of being grateful to the powers vested in you from above. With this deception in your mind, you tend to suppress others and create an aura of domination and negative manifestation further leading to lower levels of self-esteem and incredulity. Pride and malevolence add another layer of horrendous appearance to your personality owing to which you start losing your capacity of being a miracle-worker thus obliterating all the successful milestones you had achieved in your life.

Imagine yourself being an inventor of something which has never been thought of. Now it is not just you who worked for the invention. You might have a team working with and for you, your friends and family with their steadfast support and trust in you, your sibling or your spouse praying for your success. But eventually you consider yourself to be the sole-worker which makes you stand in a dense fog of narcissism, transforming you into a megalomaniac whose delusional thinking makes him believe that he is the ultimate power. With this huge delusion, you forget others' due diligence hence you are wrapped in a shawl of condescending attitude. You tend to stop thinking of others as worthy even to talk to. So eventually you grind alone and eventually the moment arrives when even if you burn the midnight oil, everything goes in vain. This is when your self-esteem hits you hard in the groin and all the powers vested in you leave a void. Devoid of divine powers you feel worthless.

The cycle of destruction becomes incessant if you are unable to overcome your narcissistic attitude.

As a consequence, you tend to remain aloof, with no friends to hang out with. In such dire times, again, you curse others instead of controlling yourself. While starting the cycle of vengeance you must remember that karma hits hard. What you give, comes back manifold- be it a blessing or a curse. In such situations when your mind remains uncontrolled and moves unceasingly, you can undergo chronic diseases or even a destructive life. Your health, especially your mental health takes a deep dive south. Descending the ladder of success is not a child's play. And if the person undergoing this horrid trauma is a megalomaniac, it becomes a matter of life and death.

All in all the self-doubt pervades further obliterating any divinity left inside thus leaving you less than average, you start finding the scapegoat to play blame-game for your downfall and spend the rest of the life in an unfathomable gorge.

Karmic Alignment

As the word suggests, karma in other words means the past deeds or the deeds which one has performed in the previous births hence everyone has to bear the consequences, whether good or bad.

The ones under the 1st Karmic Alignment number had already been at the highest pedestal of their spiritual and mental development yet they fell into an abyss of ego-centrism, hence in this birth they indubitably have a massive potential in both spiritual and material realms but they need to tread another path devoid of ego and pride to achieve salvation.

If you are under the negative influence of the 1st Karmic Alignment number, you must be apprehensive of the people around you hence a loner. Generally one can succeed with teamwork, inspiration from others and definitely a pat on the shoulders by the family. Thus you must acknowledge that your apprehensiveness shall cost you much more than being a loner, a failure maybe. It is definitely up to whether you would like to sit and work out your plans with someone or not. The relationships with others will enforce a positive impact on your work, thus you shall be able to comprehend the organizational skills more efficiently. You are a leader by birth and if the leader becomes a loner, whom would he lead? Therefore, it is imperative for you to understand that you must control your aggressive policies and principles in life so that you can put forth your leadership skills in order to help others' find their paths while keeping your control altogether.

Bringing the flexibility in your character, you can upscale your tasks in a jiffy. But an irrefutable fact is that you ought to be selfless in certain matters. A leader doesn't argue on petty issues thus you must learn to let go of what would not matter much and let others take control to exhibit the benevolence and generosity of a leader which makes you an example to follow.

The word Magician truly belongs to you owing to the capacity to amalgamate the divine and material while churning out the benefits for yourself and for others around you. In fact, your destiny is to become a miracle-worker as you can deftly create and manipulate situations around you to reap benefits.

Being a perfectionist, you are certainly prone to stress and anxiety. Nothing is perfect in this world, you must understand. Once you start appreciating your flaws, you would bring your anxiety to a halt. The best way to annihilate this demon of anxiety is to meditate. Meditation would bring your divinity out, helping you to understand what matters the most in life. Nothing is far more important than being selfless and content.

Another way to nip the evil bud of stress is to go with the flow. Life tends to puts us all in directions which may seem tough at first but are instead a blessing in disguise. So you can let the life guide, without any rebellious thoughts or actions. Keep walking in directions unknown to you while treading absolutely new paths which will lead to eventually what you had been yearning for. Spend more time in nature for you will experience bliss.

As the adage goes, 'Action speaks louder than words' hence you must act in order to achieve what you aim rather than contemplating what should be done and what not. Plans only brought to fruition only if you are passionate about your work. Your passion demands creativity and you, my dear, are brimming with creative juices. So let them flow.

Since you have been gifted with wizardly qualities, you ought to be able to recognize the higher energies working around you to make your life miraculous. Never limit but learn to control your thought-process and develop your optimism to manifest your dreams into reality.

You are a miracle-worker. Your body is a temple and the temple is a place where purity resides so you must practice everything which coincides with purity such as meditation, prayers, rituals, staying in nature and whatever makes you feel closer to your divine guardian angels. If you ever come across any doubt, leave everything as it is and align with the ultimate power through meditation.

You are a magician. You can do wonders. Everything around you works miraculously. Hence you must remain stress-free because everything will fall into its place after all.

Affirmation

I am a magician, a juggler who can juggle many tasks with efficiency at the same time. I can do wonders to make my life and the lives of others around me beautiful and harmonious. The divine powers in me makes me a magnet of love, kindness and miracles. I bow down to my innate powers. My gratitude knows no bounds.

2
THE HIGH PRIESTESS

Introduction

An epitome of intuition and mystery, the 2nd Karmic Alignment number entails the unfathomable feminine energy. Directly associated with the Moon as per the astrological significance, the female draws attention towards the whirlwind in the mind. The amalgamation of unconscious and sub-conscious minds, the clashes between them and the irreplaceable gap is represented by the female in blue. The hidden aspects of the mind are tapped when this karmic number is in power.

Introspection is what the 2nd karma number screams. While balancing the worlds, balancing the mind is left behind and this is what the feminine focuses at. This channel of energy ensures that the inherent has the capacity to balance between the dark and light. This can be interpreted as spiritual and material or good and bad. Once introspection is spot on, relying on the intuition becomes easy.

Intuitive powers are what every single person is endowed with yet hardly a fraction knows how to put it to use so the karmic alignment number 2nd here aides the inherent to follow their intuition rather than placing their faith solely on logic and reasoning. It can be transcreated as the wisdom of infinite mysterious possibilities leading to an abyss of secrets.

'Go within' is the thematic interpretation of the 2nd Karmic Alignment number in the matrix.

Positive Characteristics

The people with 2nd Karmic Alignment number are often regarded as the ones with affinity for everyone. Being a mediator, once their presence is recognised in a conflict, the matters get resolved in minutes. While ensuring that everyone around them remains intact with harmony and prosperity, they tend to reallocate these energies to those who need it the most.

If you are one of those under the 2nd number of Karma, you have the superpower of popping the bubbles of extreme emotions and letting the air to settle. Since you have that diplomatic capacity to shut down the conflicts easily, you are known as a peacemaker.

Learning new things every day is in your blood. It is as if you survive and thrive on new information whether it is related to knowledge, politics or any other matter. You definitely have countless friends. Owing to your selfless love and harmonious nature towards your allies, you are popular amongst them anyway, isn't it?

With an extreme sense of caution, you pry. You are an observant rather than a teller. You, born with a charm of mystery, are able to demystify the hidden faces behind. Whether it is your brain or your sixth sense but somehow you get to know what is going on behind those clandestine doors, despairingly happy faces and simple yet enigmatic tricks? You know that everything comes for a price in this world so you don't fall a prey to those who offer themselves to you without any demands at first.

A healer by nature, you tend to everyone in need-be it an elder on the crossroads, a kitten stuck in a tree branch or a teen struggling in life. You are a go-to for many of your friends and acquaintances. Your faculties to solve the problems, relieve others from pain-be it literal or metaphorical, or to calm somebody in a difficult situation is what comes to you effortlessly.

While you are composed of endless leadership skills, you always remain behind the curtains of innocence. It seems like you avoid showing your real life-saving skills to the world. With you as a leader, many would bolster in their lives however you tend to give others the chance to shine but you often remain unattached to fame and hardly ever take any credit for your due respect and help. You simply choose to inspire rather than to lead others. You forge paths for others while convincing them that they did it themselves. You are what a selfless person should be. You epitomise the selflessness in this world.

While helping out others, you ensure that your courtyard doesn't get muddy with slander. You care thoroughly for your personal space and if you feel that someone might threaten your meditative space then you scratch their names from your mental diary and let them go instead of stretching the matter. All in all, avoiding conflicts is what you believe in.

Balancing on the tip of a needle is another part of your nature. You always maintain your mental and emotional equilibrium no matter what the circumstances are. With your love towards nature, you already are aware of the importance and pertinence of balance in life so you lead others towards it along with yourself.

Negative Characteristics

The negative influence of the 2nd Karmic Alignment number is the exact opposite of how an inherent is or behaves under the positive influence. With such a striking difference, the inherent is unable to mitigate in the right way possible. When you enter into your negative manifestation, the tables turn and you become the one creating illusions and conflicts. Also becoming popular as a back-stabber, you start losing allies, turning them into your foes.

Distorting information to let others go haywire starts to get aligned in your life as if it was never absent. Not only unreliable, but you with your actions also ensure that others start doubting your abilities. You start diplomacy in the negative light hence you are also called a hypocrite for maintaining standards differently for yourself and for others.

Imagine how someone can keep smiling at you while stabbing your back and sawing your support without batting an eyelid. With no regrets in life, you tend to become this malevolent and violent person who is ever ready to manipulate facts to create discord between anyone and everyone. As you despise the loneliness, you somehow find your match and then you both work in pair.

You epitomise gas-lighting. With what seems like a psychological disorder, you say one thing, confess another and believe in something differently. With you as a business partner, one should be cautious because you tend to change statements like changing clothes. Illusionary legend, you can create the 'chakravuhya' for others. The way out is unknown even to you but you do it just for fun which sometimes may cost others' their lives.

People can easily fall a prey to your potential of manipulation multiple times. You are flawless when it comes to diplomacy. If your positive manifestation helps you to reveal the secret desires of others, just imagine for once how good you would be in distorting their emotions. Dishonesty is what you live for during these times. You can go to any lengths to achieve what you aim for.

You keep on cribbing about how bad everything is, how useless everyone else is but you would not even think of working on yourself even once. You think of yourself as someone with an impeccable character but in reality you become nothing short of a cry baby with no sense of accountability or maturity.

Balancing becomes a huge task for you. A gossip generator, you fall into the trap of materialistic obsessions with no way out. While sitting on the fence as your negative conditioning, you become weak-willed and are unable to show your personality traits according to your gender.

In a nutshell, you become the worst version of your positive manifestation but you must not forget that what you give to the universe comes back a hundred-fold. Don't forget that if you perform such deeds incessantly, then you can also become a backstage conversational topic even for your subordinates.

Karmic Alignment

People under the 2nd Karmic number are best cultivated when they rest their logic and trust their intuition. Their intuition powers are extremely steadfast yet they fall a prey to reasoning.

If you fall under this category then you already know how introspection helps you, whether you do it willingly or forcibly. Introspection helps you to feel calm, relaxed, to understand what goes between the crevices of a linear mind. You must get above board with yourself. Being honest with someone else is one thing, but looking at yourself in the mirror with bare eyes of honesty and conviction is a task many heroes fail to perform. But you must. You ought to be the hero of your life. You ought to be an epitome of wisdom and honesty because that is what your soul knows. Honesty and integrity is what you inner self is made up of. The rest of the superficial layers have been added by the world. Peel them one by one.

For starters, trust others. Start by taking baby steps. Not everyone wants your slice of cake. If you may notice, someone is looking at you to know if you want another slice and help you accordingly. Keep that positive approach towards everyone. Don't let your guard down suddenly but you must understand how imperative it is for you to love others and yourself. Enough with being so strict and aggressive with yourself. Break free of these shackles.

In case you feel restrained, go out. Go on a walk. Exercise. Move your body. The more you move your body, the less restrained you would feel. Open your heart towards the voiceless. Be kind to them.

Refrain from doubting yourself and the universe. The universe is at your disposal. You may wish and it will be granted only if you put trust in your wishes. Shower others with your wisdom. Don't hold back when it comes to giving as what you give, you receive manifold.

'For whatever a man sow, this he will also reap' henceforth you must sow the seeds of kindness and goodness wherever you put forth your foot. And save the pearls of wisdom you get from others. Treat yourself and others with respect and attention. The more you take care of yourself, the better your holistic health will be and eventually you will be full of vigour, happiness and prosperity.

Upbringing of your intuitive abilities can further enhance your sense of well-being and the same can also aid in your uniquely built healing qualities.

Affirmation:

I am a healer. I heal myself and others with respect and care. My intuitive powers help me to navigate through life. I trust my instincts and work on their cues. My guardian angel Moon is the reason behind my calm and composed mind. I am grateful to the high powers for blessing me with love, kindness and clarity.

3

THE EMPRESS

Introduction

The 3rd Karmic Alignment number is all about a lady of royalty, symbolising fertility through her feminine archetypes. The queen, sitting on a red throne depicts the ever flowing aspects of fertility. An archetype of motherhood, the dress of the Fertility Queen is full of pomegranates which also symbolise divine femininity.

The number deals with the growth and expansion-be it business, studies, or a matter of conceiving. The karma number is a positive bracket within which even if the dust is touched it can turn into gold. The Enchantress has a direct connection with the Fertility Queen owing to the river. The flow of water is till prevalent in this Karmic Alignment number thus the flow of creativity must never halt.

With the depiction of 12 stars, the 12 apostles are symbolic of 12 zodiac signs in astrology. Further this code is directly in relation with the planet Venus, the luxurious and royal traits are present during the period of this Karmic number. If the marriage is on the rocks, this code exhibits the positivity. Likewise, conceiving any ideas or making plans can lead to fruitful results during this spectacular period.

While nature is a sign of abundance, this Karmic number also enunciates the fact that life is a beautiful journey to be spent in luxury and with love.

Positive Characteristics

Since the people leading the lives of 3rd Karmic Alignment number are under the direct influence of fertile and creative powers and prowess, they tend to be the influencers and managers. With exceptional organizational skills, they are able to prioritise between family, professional life and also the social recognition. They are adept in finding ways to earn money and to run their business independently.

If you are a lady with 3rd Karmic Alignment number, you are the true queen in terms of royalty, exuberating and nurturing factor. With unprecedented femininity, you keep the nature in order. With a wonderful taste in beauty and a passion for luxury, you are always in a calm and composed orderly way of life.

If you yourself are this empress then you must be aware about how well you balance your time and effort between yourself and devoting time to your family too. You never put yourself down for anything may happen. The other sex is attracted to you owing to this virtue of yours. Your beauty is unmatchable.

In other words, you have magnetic powers for men as well as money. These get attracted to you like an infant to his mother-undivided attention and craving for you. Not only you are beautiful but you also know how to enhance your beauty with your appearance, your ways of putting yourself out there in the dark and wild with grace which is an exceptional quality only present in a handful.

Once you attract wealth, you become more generous than ever without even realising. You tend to start enjoying the wealth with others in much need which makes you a benevolent person too. With this attitude towards life, you attract everything a woman can desire for. Even the leadership skills seem innate to you thus you become a leader with a title. You are an epitome of how a queen leads. Be it the role of fighting for the right ways and leading others in the virtuous ways in the conference rooms or hosting a party at your home, you always are impeccable. You are an organizer and a preserver.

Now you yourself are a cream of the crop hence you attract the man brimming with the qualities of a king. What makes him a king is your attitude towards him, which is truly appreciative such as remaining loyal to him ever and always, to not only give him due respect and importance but also put emphasis on his strength and endeavours. Even in the direst of circumstances, you remain unaffected and love him from the core of your heart which makes you a queen through and through.

Only persons with higher frequencies get in your life, attract to you and love you and get loved by you. You become truly one of a kind when you are under the 3rd Karmic Alignment number. Gradually you turn into a goddess, figuratively, as you tend to maintain the equilibrium between the queen and the homemaker.

The Karmic Number is a feminine one so everything a female has innately is acquired by the men when they come under the influence of the 3rd Karmic number in their lives. With their motherly touch, they can become great educators for small children. They can also create a place for themselves in the field of child fashion and cooking as well.

If you are one of those men who are passionate about the right way to cook and clean, then you are indubitably going through a period of 3rd Karmic Alignment number. You are one of those who would give friendly advice to other women how to cook and keep an orderly way of life. If someone wants to know what a woman wants, you are a go-to person. As you know what a woman wants from a man's perspective, it becomes a cake walk to lead a married life. You become the favourite son of your mother. You are a father that daughters only hear about-such perfection to an extent that you make the women in your life feel lucky to have you.

As a man, you know how to strike a balance between the relationship of the mother and wife. Owing to this fact, you lead a stress-free life, a harmonious life which is a far cry for other men with married lives. However you are extremely vulnerable to the atrocities life throws at you. In times of death or divorce, you break down and it takes a lot of time for you to get back on track. You are hyper-sensitive, not that it is wrong in any way, but it makes your yearn security at all times so you keep giving to others in order to keep them satiated with your prowess.

In order to hide your innate feminine nature, you tend to put on the mask of being muscular and stronger. You put on fake appearances but only your near ones know how beautiful your soul is.

You learn to be responsible gradually. You can make a great leader if the field is related to beauty.

Negative Characteristics

The character takes a sharp turn with the negative manifestation when it comes to women.

If you are that woman, whose personality is affected with the negativity of the 3rd Karmic Alignment number, beware of your controlling and condescending attitude.

You believe in doing everything for yourself and your near ones all by yourself just because you think that nobody else can do it in a better way which may seem normal sometimes but looks absurd when it starts to become your obsession because at the end of the day, you cannot do everything all by yourself. It's practically impossible.

You have a hard time in delegating your duties which makes your job less effective and more stressful. With your fist tightly closed, nobody likes to get near you. Especially the men, they feel repelled to do so. Likewise, you feel that there is a dearth of good men around you. You find faults in everything the men near you do. You keep a capricious attitude towards them and when you are unable to retain relationships, you blame the other gender. Owing to this, your married life also turns chaotic and messy with arguments, fights, and unresolved mental battles which give birth to negative energies in the relationship thus you tend to focus more on your career rather than give due importance to family building and when time flies, you regret of being quite late in starting in family.

Money becomes the core essence of your being in terms of negative manifestation. You hoard it. You keep it locked away. The more you earn, the more of a penny picker you become. You are in constant need of money however you hardly spend anything on yourself or others. So your materialistic realm is unaligned to an extent that you can never achieve that much success you yearn for because your energies are in the wrong direction.

With such inflexible and controlling attitude, you tend to lose your aspect of leading. Your greed for fame, name and money increases and starts getting jealous of the women who have better lives than you.

The men going through such negative manifestation of 3rd Karmic Alignment number tend to have their masculinity falter when it comes to decision-making which has dire consequences so instead of getting over with it, they sit on the fence and keep on contemplating.

If you are one of those men, you may know that you tend to become effeminate when the situation requires a manly attitude, only if you are uninterested. You like to act as per the apron strings of your wife because you feel confident in her lap rather than keeping her safe. You can call yourself a ladies' man yet you tend to become submissive to all the women in your life whether they deserve your love and submission or not. You start doing it habitually. You become prone to such women who take you for granted. It can be your mother, your sister or your wife or even your daughter.

And due to this, you may feel dejected as you start despising women. So eventually you may end up as someone who likes women who fight for you. You take out your petty acts on women out of your rebellious attitude. You may start a competition of winning you over for them and may watch them cat-fighting to get you.

Money is a constant reminder for you to get better however since your personality lacks courage, discipline and the attitude to handle high positions in society, you tend to lose even your generational wealth bit by bit which makes you completely out of tune. You can earn as much as you want however you must put yourself out there.

You must understand the value of balancing the tip of scales when it comes to being masculine as well as feminine.

Karmic Alignment

Masculinity and femininity are two aspects which must complement each other. If a male becomes overly feminine, he is regarded as effeminate. On other hand, a lady when acts muscular, she is termed manly. So an equilibrium must be maintained between the two because none can survive without the other and in case if he/she tries to, then it leads to mental chaos.

For the men, the perfect advice is to start respecting the women present in their lives. If you are a man with 3rd Karmic Alignment number in order, you must become accountable for your actions without any ulterior motives. You ought to respect your female counterpart present in your life with dignity, respect and should trust their instincts for once when it comes to decision-making. Doubting the ladies in your life will lead you nowhere. In fact, you would remain aloof.

You are the good guy inside out but the world doesn't treat the good guys exceptionally. The ways of the world are crooked. The world and the worldly people believe in just one rule-hunt or be hunted. Consequently, you must learn to earn name, fame and money by following the rules of the worldly affairs instead of being above board always.

Your resilience will pay you manifold only if you show the courage to stand against the ill and take the necessary steps.

In these contemporary times, the women are putting equal efforts in almost every field physically possible. However, with this Karmic number, the ladies are more dominant rather than playing an equal. They must avoid being a stinger, figuratively.

If you are a lady with 3rd Karmic Alignment number in your life, you must comprehend that equilibrium is of essence. Refrain from suppressing the opposite sex for your personal gains. You ought to cut him/them a slack by bringing some range of flexibility in your life. Not the only the opposite sex but also everybody who is in your immediate circle. You need to understand that incorporating such dominant beliefs can hamper your growth.

Keep your attitude healthy towards money. Avoid being penny pinching. It cannot take you far ahead.

Your control is important, sometimes it is inevitable but do you control the plane you are sitting in while flying from your nation to your dream destination? Do you know how well trained the pilot is? Or do you enquire about the crew members who would stay with you throughout the flight? No, you simply trust the Lord and let it be. So why can't you act the same towards your family and close friends? Why do you always have to be so coercive to an extent that they should call you narcissistic?

You have divine powers of abundance. You must understand that the God is everywhere and he is taking care of you, your close ones and even the ones who you don't know yet. The whole world is under his control so you needn't worry about anything. You have ample confidence, isn't it? You epitomise beauty and order. Think about the ones who just dream of it. Aren't you lucky? Relax and let go of all the worries, fears and blocks in your mind and heart.

Once you stop controlling, everything around will bloom. Your spouse is ready to put the whole world at your feet, you just need to be open to him. Your children will show you the exemplary world if you loosen your control.

Look after your appearance. You are beautiful inside out. But grooming a bit won't hamper anything, would it? Beautify yourself and your surroundings. Stay well-dressed. Respect yourself. Respect other women. Spend your time luxuriously. If your life is luxurious already, then you must enjoy every bit of it to attract more. In case you are struggling to get the luxuries in life, you must remain grateful for what you have and enjoy every bit of it to the fullest.

The more grateful you are, the more divinity and luxuries will enter your being. You are not meant for discussing petty issues and household chores but for bigger things. You can lead and you must. All you have to do is devote your time to yourself, your family and then you will realise how worthy your life is.

Affirmation

I am the sole creator of my destiny hence abundance flows in me. My one touch can turn dust to gold. I am grateful for the divine powers of nurturing myself as well as others. My creativity knows no bounds. My life is as luxurious and royal as the kings and queens.

4
THE EMPEROR

Introduction

The 4th Karmic Alignment number is all set to teach stability through masculine energies. An epitome of authority and power, this Karmic number engages the inherent in keeping structure and order to bring stability in his/her life to feel secure.

The Green-man is a masculine energy, symbolizing fatherhood. The archetypal translation is of an old wise man indicating the value of discipline and organizational skills while establishing clear boundaries. Everything comes handy in taking some prominent decisions as the masculine energy encourages to believe in logic rather than emotion. Quite rational in all the aspects, the green-man personifies a leader with strong and confident goals who considers himself accountable for all he has done.

As per the astrological connection, the emperor or the green-man is in direct relation to the planet Mars. Also the whole Karma number is related to the 'rajas guna' which is all about action, velocity and acceleration.

The eye-catching factor is that the water flowing from the High Priestess can be seen in this Karmic number as well. That means the creativity is never meant to come to a halt. With the assertiveness in mind, one can gather the courage and strength to go beyond the reaches of an average mind and achieve what has never been achieved before in the history of mankind. Everything mentioned above can be done while connecting oneself to the strong male figures in life since this Karmic number is a masculine energy solely.

Positive Characteristics

If you are a woman who has 4th Karmic Alignment number in her matrix currently, you are an example for other women in your life to start and retain the relationships on the right foot with all the men in life whether in a father-daughter duo, husband-wife or brother-sister. Since your relationship with your father has been an epitome of relationships with the opposite sex, it has become a great cornerstone for your other relationships in life.

Sometimes when one feel they have every virtue others dream of, they start taking it all for granted. Likewise, you are a strong-willed woman with a great acumen for every field you enter in, hence you also take your prowess of retaining relationships for granted. It seems like it never really occurred to you how to use these superficial traits of yours.

You are one of a kind when it comes to negotiating in business deals, or mastering any sort of situation when someone or you yourself are in a fix. In fact, you can easily start your own business and perform exceptionally well in it.

You ought to understand that you are brimming with the masculine energies during the Karmic Alignment number 4th hence you need to lower down your manliness. It is hard to understand but you must get softer in your approach. Apart from the mental changes, you can start bringing changes to your personality which can further strengthen the fact that you are inclined towards the masculine energy. Short hair, sporty style, engaging in activities meant mainly for men and choosing the career options which are more suitable to men.

You cannot understand now how difficult it will be to overcome it all however you are supposed to control your emotions and desires for your betterment in the coming future.

If you are a man with 4th Karmic Alignment number in your charts, it is time that you become accountable and responsible in your approach towards everyone. Your life is full of opportunities and possibilities to ascend towards the pinnacles of success during this particular period.

You have an innate ability of disciplining yourself without any effort along with impeccable organizational skills. Delegating the tasks, or doing them in an orderly manner is what makes you a great organizer in this matrix. If you have started anything such as a business, a project or a work which is heavy duty, during this period you must put your heart and soul in finishing it.

So much obsessed with work, you forget that you need to rest too. You may seem cold towards yourself as you prefer staying emotionless. However you fulfil all the desires and needs of your family members without fail. You may feel happy, but your face and body stay still. Observe yourself and you shall know how focused you are in your work that the rest of your feelings come to a halt while being expressed.

You step up easily in the matters of structural order, especially the political matters. Not only you get attracted towards such matters but you also succeed. With logic and reasoning, you come up with endeavours and ideas which may seem flabbergasting at first but others start understanding your approach gradually and you become their leader due to your innate capacities to lead others without any restraint.

Imagine yourself as a man of steel. Nothing can break you, slay you or hurt you metaphorically. You have such strong qualities stirs up that strength, determination, acumen, diligence-everything comes naturally to you.

You as a family man are a perfect package. With no drama involved, all problems at bay, you tend to your family in the best possible manner. Your parents as well as your children are always on cloud nine with your love towards them. You bestow them love through ways which are spectacular.

Negative Characteristics

With the masculine Karmic number at some point in life, the women become threatening in ways which may seem horrendous to men. Once or twice a woman can go through feelings for men but not every day for a period of time. It imbalances the role of women at home as well as at their workplace.

If you are one of those woman, who is going through the 4th Karmic Alignment number, you ought to understand that there cannot be two men in an equal relationship with you also acting as if you are the dominant self. You tend to become someone who starts attracting immature and weak men in your life, in your house, your office or your life in general. This makes you more belligerent and intolerant for others. It is simply not possible for you to handle both the womanly and manly aspect in the household. However even then, you dominate your man at home, push him to an extent that he starts earning less, becomes less competitive at his workplace or tends to lose his prestige or maybe stop working at all.

In a relationship, you also are accountable and responsible for your actions. It is not the sole responsibility of the man of the house to handle all the conflicts by himself, the conflicts created by you especially. So you are at a loss if you think you are the ruler of your house because your husband might have to take the softer approach which in the long run can hamper the mental growth in ways undetermined. You are setting the wrong example for your children too.

Living a life of belligerence when your anger is always on the tip of your nose, you tend to keep fighting with your husband. Going through such circumstances is quite natural for you as you are going through the 4th Karmic Alignment number however it makes your man incapable of leading life peacefully. He does not know the reason behind the cat and dog life you both are leading. With no fault of his, he is still forced to comply to your relentless approach of fighting back. At times, these men also lose their temper. You cannot and should not always test his patience. What if he resorts to domestic violence? What if he takes on the manly approach all of a sudden to an extreme level and then you become helpless. You must loosen up your strangle. Eventually your nature to strangle him will vanish.

There are other scenarios when you may feel that you have been friend-zoned in all your potential relationships. Owing to your belligerence, your pugnacious attitude towards men, or the manly approach in physical attributes, you become a potential go-to friend for the one/ones whom you believe to be your beau. You may have dreamt of them as being your boyfriend/husband but imagine them asking you for a friendly advice to impress or propose their crush. How hurtful it can be! In other words, just because you are a female by sex does not make you a female. You need to look like one. You need to become soft in your approach.

Some men can become alcoholics, thanks to their wives who are always on the nagging mode no matter what the circumstances are. The best way to forget an eternally dissatisfied wife is a glass of wine. Are you one of these women who is always in demand for more, or is cribbing for attention? Relax yourself. Cut your man some slack. He has a life of his own. Let him be.

Even if you are providing financial support to the family, are you giving your husband the personal attention that he is obliged to? Are you drifting away from him day by day? Does he come anywhere near your ambitious life? If the answer is debatable, then put yourself in his shoes for a minute and think what would you do to satiate yourself? You got the answer right. Cheating is what he would do instead of the long-awaited love of yours.

You, as a woman are supposed to be the one to give shoulder to your man just like he is supposed to. But if also try to become another man in the relationship, how would it succeed? You must focus on the relationships in your life. It is imperative. It may sound ludicrous now but think about it time and again that if you are handling any of the familial responsibilities or ignoring them altogether then what would become of you?

If you are a man leading the 4th Karmic Alignment number in your charts, you have totally forgotten that what you give to the nature, it comes back a hundred-fold. Your cruelty knows no bounds. Imagine yourself getting the taste of your own medicine, would you like it?

Such authoritarianism. You have become a dictator in the lives of your subordinates at work and in your home too. Everybody is afraid of you and you think they all respect you?

Exhibiting such control over your family members may force them to despise your presence at home which can make the matters go bad to worse.

Your arrogance is at its pinnacle. Not only your children can follow in your footsteps, but even your wife can become belligerent to some extent if you don't change your ways.

At your workplace, you are considered a Scrooge with an eternal long angry face. Not accepting anyone's disposition, always forcing others to take your opinion as the best and ensuring that everyone is in your control makes you a Scrooge. You have become as selfish as a man can be.

Try to understand, sometimes you got to give back or return the favours. You are not obliged to take away everything from others. Their peace of mind, their ambitions, their lives too. Observe how people feel in your presence and look out how the same set of people feel when they think you are absent from that situation.

Your relations with your fathers are strained but that does not mean that you have to do the same with your son too.

Wake up from this tyrannical dream and soften your approach towards all near you.

Karmic Alignment

With ever-flowing masculine energy, this Karmic number brims with the masculinity and authority.

If you are a woman with the 4th Karmic Alignment number in your chart, then you must realise that you are controlling every man in your vicinity which is definitely not a good thing to do. You must trust the men in your life, be it your father, husband or son. Not everybody is the same. You must not generalise every man as dominant or a control freak because this perception of yours is repelling all the men from your life.

You ought to stop interfering in the matters related to others. You must remain in your boundaries if you want to keep good relations. Being manly is not a vice but you yourself are proving that you have lost the feminine touch owing to which your softness has come to an end.

It is comprehensible that someone has hurt you, but misdirecting your anger on others is what you are doing time and again. You must learn to forgive. You must learn to let go. Go with the flow as they say because every time you just cannot tighten up. Eventually you will lose yourself if this controlling attitude stays.

If you are a man with 4th Karmic Alignment number in your chart, by now you must have experienced how you feel for the fairer sex. You are a protector by nature. You are supposed to be the cane to support the women in your life, be it your mother, sister, wife or daughter. Instead of becoming the cane, you use this cane to control them to an extent that they are scared of you. Refrain from being the villain where you should be the hero. Rather let go of the control and see how fast and beautifully they all flourish while they consider you reverend.

Another misaligned form in your chart is you obsess over money. Undeniably, money is pertinent. Does that mean that you forget the structure and order or earning it? Does that mean you start suppressing others for your benefit? Does it mean you are privileged to take unfairly from others?

Nature has a rule-what you give you receive manifold. And you, on the other hand have no intention of giving but instead you are focused on hoarding wealth. You have enough. You have more than what is required. Start donating to the ones in need. It is your hard-earned money but if a fraction of it is given in charity, it won't really make a difference in your wealth.

You are brimming with fire. The basic purpose of fire is to give warmth but instead you burn others with your criticism. Refrain from being so overly confident.

Your mission on earth is to carry the light of fairness and justice while being kind and peaceful. Hence, be the peace-maker, the light-bearer and the man of steel with benevolence.

Affirmation

I am a leader. I am in harmony with what and who I am. My energies are being channelled in the right direction. My strength and confidence is growing by leaps and bounds. I am grateful for all I have and I am.

5

THE HIEROPHANT

Introduction

When the traditions and conformity to established rules and regulations come orderly, it indicates that the revealer of the sacred is in his working zone. The societal norms, culture and heritage are given the highest pedestal, the 5th Karmic Alignment number, the revealer proves his magic. He works in the form of a teacher, an old man, a mentor or a religious leader to let the inherent walk the path of learning and seeking wisdom.

Sometimes a serious turn is taken toward the religion and the religious activities. Basically a search for personal philosophy is what derives the seer to bridge the gap between the spirit and the matter.

In the pursuit of knowledge and understanding, sometimes the seer turns into a narrow-minded individual thus becoming inflexible in relation to religion, a fanatic in simple terms. Further leading to stagnation and complacency.

As per the astrological context, Venus is the ruling planet of the revealer of the sacred. There are a couple of keys to heaven which convey that there should always be a need for spiritual purpose in life. Unless there is a desire for the same, one can fall into the trap of giving away too much power and staying a conservative traditionalist.

Positive Characteristics

The people falling under the 5th Karmic Alignment number are basically the go-to person and perfectionists. They like to design everything according to their own preferences. They set the rules of the game, makes them easy and accessible for everyone to follow and they themselves follow those rules religiously.

If you also come in this category of Karmic number during some period in your lifetime, you must consider yourself a perfectionist as what you do sets an example for others to follow. You do what a family man must, an employee is supposed to do and a human in general ought to.

Professionally, your work is impeccable. With everything spot on, you become the favourite of your employers. With your delegation of duties and no extra pressure on others, you also become a dream-like senior for your subordinates.

You follow the family customs and traditions religiously without questioning anyone's ability. To you, living for the family, raising one with morals is the most important task of your life. You live for it. You yearn for it. And when the time comes, you epitomise what one must become. Hence you set the right example for your children and they try to tread the same path as yours. Even your family supports you in all your endeavour.

You stay a student throughout your life. Be it anything that life throws at you, you take it in your stride and win over the obstacles in life. You learn, you read, you test yourself, you let others test you. All in all you are that sponge which absorbs everything and when asked to give back, you give the knowledge in a refined manner. Your approach towards life is what everyone must follow- What you sow, so shall you reap.

You are an exemplified orator. Your forte lies in logic and reasoning when it comes to dealing in business. You are a leader leading in the green room and then transforming into a follower on stage however everyone by then knows how capable and able you are to lead.

Your chosen profession are law and order, teaching, preaching and research. You tend to fall in one of these categories owing to the virtues you hold tight to.

Responsibility, accountability and dignity is what you are famous for in your inner and outer circles of social life. You believe in being fair and square to all. In family life too, you hold everything close to you in the positive sense. You love tidiness as you believe Cleanliness leads to Godliness. You have a particular style statement which is liked by everyone.

With a habit of finding logic in every part of life, you tend to become more rational than required. Sometimes you ought to flow with the flow. Sometimes you must find the spirit of the doing rather than the matter. Look up to the invisible divine energies present around you for all the answers. With this virtue, you can broaden your horizons and can easily become a preacher or a life coach.

You conduct information for others and not just give away the leaflets. Mind the difference. People like you become the trendsetters, the pioneers of newly organized tasks and ideas. As soon as you conceive an idea, it becomes apart for you to implement that idea in your being hence you create, you act and you succeed.

Negative Characteristics

You become the negative manifestation if you think that there are two viewpoints; mine and the baseless one. If you have entered the 5th Karmic Alignment number with this energy, then you must know that you repel everyone around you. People feel threatened in your presence.

Forcing your opinions on others is not only considered rude but if you turn violent while doing so, you may come across as an unlawful person too. It is understandable that you have a logical mind, but you just cannot become aggressive on the basis of what you think for it is not imperative that you are always right in every aspect and matter.

Even in family life, you tend draw boundaries for others to live and you yourself violate those boundaries by becoming a control-freak. Isn't that unfair? You give yourself way too much credit for what you do, hence you become complacent. Now if you think of yourself as the best, that does not mean that others are worthless, does it? You ought to understand that being full of pride brings vanity leading to chaos and disrespect.

Change with the times, will you? You cannot always remain in your bracket of life. Your children are the future. Let them explore for your violation of boundaries imprints their mind with trauma and when they are on their own, they still feel that they should be controlled. They become handicapped in their decision-making skills.

You can be a great teacher but that does not mean that everybody is supposed to walk on your treaded path. There can be other ways too. Finding faults in others makes you a person whom everybody tries to avoid at social gatherings. In this way you lose your circle of socialising, raising self-doubts for yourself and then self-deprecation. Thus you become somewhat dubious about your practices consequently drifting away from everyone.

Sharing your wisdom is one thing and forcing everyone to act according to it is another therefore you must draw a line when you think you are about to pounce on someone to accept your perception towards life as correct always.

Your habitability factor diminishes. You tend to be known as a chaotic person, mentally and physically. You lose yourself bit by bit to the mess.

Karmic Alignment

If you fall under the currents of the 5th Karmic Alignment number, complacency is your true enemy so is your over-confidence in imposing your ideas and perceptions on others. As a human being you have the capacity to transform, to develop, to learn and broaden your horizons however you start teaching others how to do it all instead of doing it for yourself and by yourself. Try to keep yourself clutter-free, literally and metaphorically.

You must let go the trait of over-confidence which forces you to tell people that no matter what the subject of conversation is, you are always in the right place. Intolerant is what you may define yourself as you refrain from listening to people and their opinions but expand your way of viewing the world. It is not that difficult as it seems. You just got to take the baby steps.

Actions speak louder than words so eat the frog, put your focus on doing rather than just preaching it. Stay calm while talking about your ideas so that others don't feel they are being implored to do what you say.

Let others put forth their opinions. There is no harm in listening to others. You do not have to do what they say but listening doesn't cost a dime, does it? Try to become patient when others speak for you may learn a thing or two from them.

Even if it comes to your family, you are controlling. Let them be. Let them do what they want for once. It may result in either good or bad decision but let them take a chance for themselves. Otherwise they may keep sitting on a fence even when their decision-making skills is impertinent.

If you are confident about one thing, teach it to others. It may work for them or it may not however you must not lose your morale. What you give is what you receive hundred-fold hence you should not ever be hesitant in delivering the good to others.

Now you are the perfect example of how the leaders work to bring out the best in others. Your accumulated knowledge should be spread far and wide. You must help others to take the path of spirituality in order to gain the heavenly luxuries in their lives.

If any child has 5th Karmic Alignment number in their charts, then it is a sign to let them know that they should live their life on their own terms. It is their life, not their parents' hence the will of the parents shouldn't matter much to them however due respect to their parents should not be compromised at any level.

If you are need of money during this Karma number, you must keep your house in an orderly fashion to attract the luxuries and wealth.

Affirmation

I am the connection between the spirit and matter hence I must enhance positivity in my character. I teach, preach and follow my religion with profound faith. I am grateful for what I am designed for and sent to Mother Earth.

6
THE LOVERS

Introduction

The Heart Twin symbolise the blissful relationships and abundance of love in life. Although the name symbolises love but the Karmic Alignment number 6 is related directly with decision-making acumen and intuition.

The 6th Karmic number suggests that one must listen to the heart first while choosing one out of many. Instead of relying solely on logic and reasoning, this Karma number exhibits to follow the intuition. The gut is the second brain so if the gut instinct tells something isn't right, it isn't right at all then.

Trust and understanding are others aspects of this specific Karmic Alignment number. Understanding leads to harmonious relationships, be it personal or professional. Even the personal beliefs and values are in direct link with the twin hearts due to the fact that every personal belief should be based on self-analysis in which the intuition plays a dominant role.

The two nude figures refer to the Yin and Yang energy who are being blessed by the angelic energies to initiate any sort of relation, familial or business. Any creative idea is also represented in this form of energy. The nudity refers to the innocence. The flames and the snake in the Garden of Eden symbolise inner consciousness.

The Karmic Number 6 is all about maintaining stability and not giving in to temptation without consulting with the second brain which is the gut.

Positive Characteristics

'Loneliness is a sin as unforgivable as hatred' is the motto of the people living the 6th Karmic Alignment number. Love, overly affection, ostentatious yet friendly are the people who fall in the category of the lovers or twin hearts.

If you are inclined towards impressing others even if it takes a lot of time, consider yourself a true patron of this code of karma. You are not only friendly, but with the gift of gab your personality is crowned with impeccable taste in fashion sense.

Resolving conflicts seems like a child's play to you owing to your diplomatic skills. You are very emotional yet you adore the sensual pleasures in life. If you are in love with someone, you will move mountains to make them happy and feel content with you. If ever they get upset with you, you lose your charm and fall at their feet for resolving the matter. You just cannot live without your beloved. Aren't you so romantic?

You are a connoisseur. Be it clothing, food and beverages or choosing art, you have an extremely refined taste which is unmatchable and unbeatable. You cannot stand anything less than beautiful. Call it your pride or your habit, but beauty attracts and entices you. You are a hoarder of beautiful things and people.

The special virtue that you hold is that you keep giving love to others without expecting anything in return. In the contemporary epoch, when everyone yearns for a give and take relationship, you on the other hand are the one who is benevolent from the core of your heart. If you haven't exchanged a few words of love with anyone throughout the day, you feel as if the day had been wasted.

If you choose something to work on, you burn midnight oil till its completion. With diligence and love you tend on work. You only work with what inspires you and encourages you to reach the pinnacles of success and you definitely succeed.

What others say matter more to you rather than what you think about yourself, is that not right? It is generally not appreciated as sometimes when others are wrong, you would agree with them deliberately just to suffice their opinion. It must have backfired too if you can relate.

Dressing unkemptly is what you despise truly. You cannot wear wrinkled night-suit, forget going to a ball in a messy look. You love attention. You are a cynosure who craves for attention from others. You make it look effortless but you tend to attract everyone's attention.

Parties and after-parties are what you live for. You prefer being the host so that you can shower others with your bedazzling choices of food and beverages along with music. You like to show-off. A pretentious being with an inferiority complex, you overdo everything that you do.

You strive for perfection. You thrive for attention. And you sustain on the energies you get from others. You are a boundless spirit brimming with love.

Negative Characteristics

If you experience that your mood swings sound a lot like 'Katy Perry's Hot and Cold' song, then you are experiencing the negative manifestation of the 6th Karmic Alignment number.

There is a fine line between loving and hating someone for you as you can become a shape-shifter, or more so a mood-shifter, from tender to tenacious, from pertinent to impertinent, from assertive to aggressive in seconds. Thus you pay for your mood swings later but heavily.

As open as you are in the positive manifestation, you turn a 180 degrees in negative by closing all the doors to your sanctum sanctorum. You prefer staying aloof. You consider yourself vulnerable even to a look.

Make-up, dressing up, going out sound pugnacious to you. But if you need to put an impression on someone, you would move out of your way to impress that soul even if it hurts you. You start living for people on their terms instead of putting your beliefs first.

You become a secret-spreader or also called rat amongst your friends. Sometimes, your friends would make fun of you while you spread a lie they told you on purpose. They would start mocking. And if the situation becomes argumentative, it hurts you day and night. It can put an imprint on your mind so much so that you keep on making plans to avenge or take revenge throughout the night and then in the morning as soon as you wake up, you text them or call them, call them names, say whatever you planned and then within seconds when your temper cools down, you become remorseful. Then comes the part of apologizing continuously. This vicious cycle goes on and on.

It becomes difficult for you to let go of someone close to you. Either you keep falling head over heels and keep losing or you date multiple partners at once and lose everyone near you. You believe in the external standards of beauty. Instead of the purifying the inner beauty, you tend to decorate and embellish the outer shell of yours and fall flat whenever someone still doesn't appreciate you.

You turn capricious and taciturn with the ones close to you without any reason. You expect everyone to be perfect and when they err, you discard the relationship altogether. To you, love is a toy. You like it for initial days and when it becomes old, you throw it away. Everyone has virtues and vices, just like you, so rather focus on accepting love with everything-be it a virtue or a vice. The world doesn't work on your terms.

Karmic Alignment

Love and be loved is what the people with the 6th Karmic Alignment number in their charts should believe in. If you are someone who is currently in the period of the heart twin, beware of the ostentatious promises of others in love. Love is ethereal and pure. In love you must accept the flaws of the beloved as much as you love the perfections. Everything cannot be up to your liking standards. Compromise is the key to success in relationships.

You are a vessel overflowing with love. You know how precious love is, how much emotions one carry in love but you cannot expect everyone to know the same. It may seem ludicrous but yes, you are a loving angel while others are kind angels or cruel ones too but the world has its own ways to live by.

Love yourself first. None can become who and what you are. You are extraordinarily beautiful. Others' opinions don't really matter if you know who you are. Open your heart to spiritual voices inside you. Start believing in your intuition. Place your trust in what you feel and you shall reap fruits of the unknown.

Nobody in this world is perfect. You must aim for the moon but don't put your life at stake if you get the stars instead. Idealism is a myth. It's a scam. Nobody should fall for it. Especially you who has the love in their blood and soul.

Talk to people. Let them know the real you, behind all that make-up. Refrain from being aloof. Your essence lies in loving others unconditionally. Trust that the real relationships exist and yours is about to start or have started already. Believe what your partner tells you. Learn to decode his actions and the real meanings behind his words. You would know the truth and the lies if any.

Refrain from being extremely dominating and submissive. Be moderate in your approach. Don't set the bar too high for anybody to achieve and not too low that you yourself stoop on your standards.

Acceptance and unconditional love should be your focus instead of idealistic relationships. Work on your inner beauty and the outer one will beautify simultaneously. Release the negativity and breathe in love, trust, intuition and angelic powers.

Affirmation

I am a lover. I breathe in love and affection. My inner beauty enhances my outer beauty. I am the life of the party. I am grateful for who I am and what I can do.

7
THE CHARIOT

Introduction

The Sacred Focus is the symbol for the vehicle of soul while the body along with the mind are its passengers. The 7th Karmic Alignment number dictates the movement of energies in the literal sense and the success of the inherent if he stays in control of the senses.

The white and black symbolise the yin and yang, or conscious and subconscious or the macro and microcosm. Also there must be the balance between the ambition and the sense of direction for higher levels of success. The man sitting in the sacred focus is a responsible person with a commanding authority however he has a strong heart to place all his secrets inside without fail. This Karmic number defines the way one thinks and acts.

A masculine number, triumph and conquest is what is being personified. Success can only be attained with the will-power to navigate through the testing times. There is always a need for self-control and discipline in order to reach the pinnacle of success.

The Karma number 7 entails the responsibility with an acumen for ample opportunities in life of the one who has this in their matrix. Moreover, with the angelic blessings, one can harness the powers and resources to achieve greater purposes in life.

Positive Characteristics

The Karmic Alignment number 7 deals in diving straightaway in a situation without any fear of failure. The Focus of the sacred signifies motion or the movement. Hence anyone with this Karmic Code tends to become overly confident and is able to achieve his goals with his strong will-power and mental discipline.

If you are someone who is currently under the 7th Karma number, you must know that you have the warrior spirit in you. Come what may you always yearn for success and are never afraid of countering any failures. You love to win or in other words winning is your passion hence you focus on one goal at a time and give your level best to achieve it. However you must plan carefully and with diligence to achieve your goals.

You are fond of being recognised socially and have the ear for praise. You must know how to make others follow you without putting any effort. This is your secret recipe towards success. You make your followers understand your goals, and push them far ahead to follow your footsteps that just with a little gesture you can ask them to perform as if it is a puppet show. How do you do it?

Only the people who believe in action rather than mere words tend to become a part of your team. You feel that you are accountable for every word you utter, every promise you make and every decision you take. And this is what the most productive people on this planet aim for in their daily lives.

As per the Karmic number, movement is your basic principle. It can be interpreted as you will be always on the go, or you shall face a lot of ups and downs, sudden ones, in your life. However your flexible attitude can let you sail through the rough seas. You respect your subordinates, you give due respect to your seniors. Moreover, you talk and act respectfully to your foes too which makes you a person with high morals.

Strengthened mind and body can help you get the desired results in terms of relationships too. You must work on your physical attributes to attract the best. Once you initiate an idea in someone's mind, it ignites with passion and ends with results. Likewise, you must plan and act upon your own ideas. Letting your team win makes you a leader but you yourself winning in life makes you a hero.

Negative Characteristics

The 7th Karmic Alignment number of negative manifestation is quite hefty as the person becomes not only lazy but aggressive and starts living a sedentary lifestyle owing to their lack of discipline.

If you are currently experiencing the 7th Karmic Alignment number, you have become extremely lazy. Off-put always, you tend to procrastinate in everything you used to excel at before. Your laziness knows no bounds now. Until and unless you start planning for your goals, you can never get off your couch. You become complacent. Stagnation clouds your mind. You ought to understand that how pertinent it is for you to set a target within a time limit to be achieved so that you can act accordingly.

You become extremely rude with others while forgetting their age or rank. How would you feel if one of your subordinates insults you before your staff? Put yourself in others' shoes whom you insult without giving a thought what they might think or what impression of your insult would put on others. You can change your behaviour by staying in your limits. When you are busy, you hardly get any time to observe others. You get engrossed in your work hence you feel your life has a meaning.

Consequently, your aggression becomes ubiquitous. This aggression can be in the form of ambitiousness, love or hatred. You overlook what is moralistic and acceptable in the society rather you become a horse with blinkers-you just cannot see what is happening around you because of your actions. By the time you achieve your goals in a time limit set by you, you are exasperated with the burden therefore you lack the enthusiasm to enjoy the sweet fruit of your success. Nobody asks you not to work but an equilibrium must be maintained between work and life. Owing to your aggression, you tend to have complicated relationships in life.

Once you are done with a goal, you feel worthless afterwards if you do not set another target. Life has bigger purposes too. The sacred focus doesn't let you feel stable without any sort of movement in life-be it literal or figurative. The energies have to be exchanged somehow. You not only consider the world your battleground but you fight to be the one who wins at any cost-even if it costs you your peace and harmony.

This inability to relax even during your pleasurable hours with family and friends makes you a snob. All work and no play makes Jack a dull boy. With this perception of life, you must bring changes to your fast forward lifestyle with no peace and quiet in between. With no place for family or any other relationships, you may feel worthless.

If you think that every favour you get from others has a tail of ulterior motive, and you must fight for every little thing in life then you are in the wrong. Life is not race because you are not a rat. You have cognitive abilities to act upon. Your conditioning might have been done to keep working but take a break. Go on a sabbatical. Explore the things which you have never even heard of. Visit those spots which were unknown to you. You can take your spouse alongside. Refrain from being controlling. Give yourself much-needed reward and a break, mentally and physically.

Your subconscious mind is always fighting battles for you. You cannot erase anything from it but you must add new interesting experiences from your life. You must understand how inevitable some problems are. Not everything is to be fought with. There will be times when life will throw bricks at you to make a castle and you with your battleground ideas would feel that life is throwing a challenge. Try to bring changes in your approach towards life and the world would become a beautiful place to live in.

Do not divide the world in black and white. The world is always grey, no matter how many times you mark it as good or bad. You are a part of grey. Even your character has flaws. Learn to forgive yourself and others. You would know when a mistake has been committed and when an act of rebellion is taking place.

Insatiable is the nature of mankind and you are no different but learn to relax. Give yourself rewards for your goals when achieved. For instance, you can take a short trip abroad if you have achieved a target over a period of a year or two. Or you can go eat an ice cream if you haven't controlled anyone during the day. As simple as that. Simplify your life and your intentions. You will feel light.

Imagine a monkey with a time bomb. How dangerous it will be for him and for the ones near him? With one wrong move, he can destroy the world for many. Consider yourself as that monkey with your subconscious mind and such behaviour as the time bomb. With one severe move, you can bring an end to your life and the lives of related to you.

Karmic Alignment

The people falling under this Karmic number are the warrior winners due to the strength they hold in themselves. If you are living with this code in your current stage, you must be familiar with the way your energies align when you help others with your strength and mental capacities. You must find your inner peace while achieving your goals as well as while helping others.

Forcing others is never the right thing to do. When you get aggressive, just remind yourself that how would you feel if someone pushes you to do something against your will. You are a leader by nature. Leaders encourage and then push forward the ones who are willing to be pushed. You must not force anyone belligerently. Laziness and indiscipline sometimes takes the toll on your nature but then that is your issue to be handled not someone else's. Hence refrain from imposing your lack of discipline on others.

Your intuitive energy is you being the light-bearer. Trust your instinct and let go of everything which becomes a hurdle between you and your destination. Your prowess lies in following your intuition. So for the sake of your soul, look at the world as a beautiful place to live in instead of cribbing about it.

The Karma number depicts the movement of energies. Use those energies for the betterment of yourself and others around you. If you aim for the moon, you shall reach it if you put your heart and soul into the task. Your systematic planning and organizational skills can come handy while fixing the blueprint of your dreams and vision. If you put the plan in place with your acumen, there is no power in this universe which can defy the orders. The universe is at your command. It is up to you whether to just keep making plans or plan and act upon it.

Meditation and sports activities can become the guiding force and an aid respectively in achieving your goals and ambitions. You must set your targets so high that you become an inspiring icon for many to follow your footsteps. Keep everyone posted about what your targets are and what you have been planning to achieve further. Your one word of wisdom can create many great lives out of it.

Start sharing your positive experiences with others. You shall notice how happy people would be to meet you, to get a glance of you to get inspired. Sharing means caring. In this context, if you share your stories of success and failure, others will act upon your advice and shall bless you with their kind words.

The purpose of your life is much higher than you think it is. With these baby steps you can achieve the targets like a cakewalk. You ought to comprehend the ways of the world, to know that you can become the star of many people's lives by letting your guard down.

Affirmation

I am grateful for the powers vested in me by the divine. My words transform into pearls of wisdom for countless. I shall achieve the greater purpose of my life. I love for who I am.

8
STRENGTH

Introduction

A symbol of personal power and resilience, the 8th Karmic Alignment number deals with self-control, fortitude and integrating the animal nature step by step. If one is able to find the inner strength and confidence in themselves then there is no force in this world which can stop him to overcome any hurdles or difficulty.

The girl taming the lion reflects symbolism which is all about the strength. One should take hold of patience and compassion in dealing with difficult situations and people owing to the fact that there are some challenges in life which need kindness and apathy instead of force and ferociousness of a lion.

The sign of infinity symbolises the paradox of self-knowledge. The more you know about yourself, the more you know that you know less. The purity of mind or innocence with the controlled desires can benefit in ways unimaginable.

It needs a lot of strength and courage to master one's emotions and control one's impulses. Hence this Karmic number brings peace and teaches to master the raw emotions to a standstill.

Positive Characteristics

If one flips the number 8 then it turns into the symbol of infinity. Hence, it can be interpreted that the Karmic Alignment number 8 deals with the past deeds and actions and one has to pay accordingly. The hidden threads of past incarnations turn into the reality of the people with 8th Karma number.

Nothing in this world happens by chance or by accident. Everything is planned according to our past karmas and actions. The people with 8th Karmic number realise this quite easily and they tend to worry less about petty issues in life. Blame-game for them ceases to exist. Everything they do is for a reason. And they also believe that everything in their lives happens for a reason.

If you come across this Karmic Alignment number in your charts, then you are undeniably accountable for your actions. Your friendliness and affection towards others is bountiful. Not only courageous enough to face the difficulties, but you also tend to plan for the foreseeable future and have a blueprint up your sleeve in case anything goes awry. With your structural approach towards every aspect in your life, you go far along.

Living life fair and square, you believe in karma so much so that you hardly ever cheat. You already know how merciless karma can be so you take only those actions which can benefit you and the ones near you. You work wonderfully as partners, be it a professional relationship or a personal one.

You happen to experience spontaneity to an extent that whether good or bad, everything returns to you within a short span of time. Since you are inclined restlessly towards the laws of the universe, the universe reverts you in ways unimaginable to others. You keep on improving yourself for the sake of your karma. You hardly ever miss a chance to work upon your habits and routine to inculcate good karma.

You are the saviour of the weak yet you tend to become high-tempered while defending them. Life is a game of the strongest therefore you cannot help each and every person who is weak because even in this scenario the past karmas are involved. For every action there is an equal and opposite reaction so you ought to understand that maybe someone who is weak in this birth may have been strong in the last one but must have done something unlawful for which he has to pay in this birth. The universe balances in its own ways which are incomprehensible to us.

You are the wisest person in your group of friends owing to which you are also popular when it comes taking advice. Everyone remains relaxed once your words of wisdom are uttered in their ears. For you, rather than the solution, the root of the problem matters more. You tend to nip the evil bud and then find the solution to the problem which shouldn't have existed in the first place.

If you choose the careers related to tax administrators or law, you shall succeed and reach the pinnacles of success. Owing to your business acumen and thinking on the spot, you are more like a conjurer with countless tricks up his sleeve.

You are a pillar of strength for many. Your way of resolving conflicts is impeccable. You tend to be that person in the family who likes to stay light headed by treading the path of truth. With your popularity in your near and dear ones, you also make great acquaintances.

Negative Characteristics

Such a drastic change occurs if the Karmic Alignment number 8 is turned upside down in the negative manifestation. The person who favours the weak becomes aggressive and finds faults with everyone he meets. Being categorical, they tend to see the world through their biased lenses.

Lose-tempered and egoistic, if you are one of those who is currently going through this karmic energy, you tend to lose the real sense and you blame others for your own doing. According to you, your failure is the result of others. The world is unfair with you only and that others are winning in life while you are losing on what you have. Your sense of perception takes a 180 degree turn with no solution in vision because you just cannot accept that even you, a mere human, can also make errors. You think of yourself as someone godly.

You attract the negative situations in your life. You become a magnet for problems, fights, legal issues, financial crisis, break-ups and what not. You ought to understand that even you can also be at wrong. You shall also have to cleanse yourself off of the mire you have soaked into.

You tend to live in a loop. You never really learn from your mistakes. Because you never accept that you made a mistake. Meanwhile your near and dear ones suffer because of your belief system. Unless you understand the law of cause and effect, life will not serve you the best. You got to accept what you give to the world. You imagine as if the whole world owes you something or the other. But you can never come face to face with the fact that maybe there is a 1% chance of you apologizing.

Karmic Alignment

Refrain from being the judge of every being who comes in contact with you. If you fall in the category of the 8th Karmic Alignment number, you should understand that there is nothing called injustice in this world. As per the karma, one has to pay for what he has done. Reaping the fruits of your own karma is something nobody can avoid in this universe. So you must balance yourself emotionally. This is a mere law of cause and effect. If you understand this law deeply, you shall never feel bad for yourself and anyone else.

You must learn the acts of kindness, acceptance, fortitude and forgiveness. Not everything needs to be handled with force. Sometimes all you need is patience and love to tame the inner devil. You must get rid of the aggression residing in your heart.

Meditation is the absolute solution to this problem. If you want to wake up the inner senses of love and benevolence in you then you must meditate and try to stay in touch with nature as many times in a day as possible. Be it gardening, or walking barefoot on grass, every act opens up new doors to inner consciousness.

Fighting small battles does not matter in the long run. Before you start arguing with someone, just think if this argument and its verdict will matter in the next 5 years in your life. If the answer is yes, then go ahead. Otherwise you know what to do in this situation. Proving your viewpoint only matters when the conversation holds the essence of law and effect. Or let it be.

Every obstacle is a blessing in disguise whether you believe it or not. Be open to learn through your mistakes for the higher powers make you err. If you ever break the balance of the karmic life, the results will be unforgivable. You will be astounded how fast the universe reacts when you take it for granted.

Just like everyone has different ice cream preferences, people have different viewpoints and everyone is right according to them. You must not act all supreme and teach them your ways. This shall give rise to provocations and tests which may prove to be destructive for you.

You are more accountable and reliable than others at your workplace but due to your negligence, you have to suffer.

Affirmation

I am well-acquainted with the laws of the universe. I know that what I shall think will be rewarded by the universe. I conceive, believe and receive for which I am ever-grateful to the divine energies residing above.

9
THE HERMIT

Introduction

The Karmic Alignment number 9 deals mainly with introspection, wisdom and healing capacities. The number basically asks for a mentorship. However with extraordinary healing powers, the Agya Chakra is activated eternally.

A time for soul-searching and self-enlightenment, this Karmic number defines that once the introspection becomes a habit, the beautiful fruits as results become a part of life. The light of knowledge and the inner truth which are symbolised by the lantern with a star means that the answers one seek are within.

To cultivate a deeper understanding of one's life and nature, one must dive into the sphere of introspection and learn the art of intuition rather than letting the logics and reasoning define their existence.

Positive Characteristics

Synonymous with wisdom, 9th Karmic Alignment number which is another term for spiritual awakening represents wise people with philosophical thought-process and healers, who heals through the art of communication. Isn't that fascinating?

If you are currently facing this Karma number or are about to enter this one in your charts, then you are in for good. With your natural flow of wisdom, you become a popular figure in your social circles as well as in your family. Your opinion is considered pertinent once someone starts following your advice. Since you believe in being slow and steady, you bring out the philosophical and logical reasoning behind every problem that people present you with, you start to bring the solutions to the problems without delving into the direct remarks. Another impression you set for the others is that you make up a story, share your anecdote or a fable to explain the solution which is absolutely out of the box sort of healing. Not only the hearts, but you also heal the souls of the people which is a lot to do. Your sense of observation and listening skills makes you patient enough to understand the problem from others' point of view.

Rather than calling it complacency, you are happy with who and what you are and the list of things that you can do. You have no complaints from yourself or from others. You not only like to read and learn new everyday but you tend to practice the scientific factor behind everything. Your choice of career can be becoming a scientist because of your inclination towards this profession. Your brain works faster than your body hence you are more capable of doing the mental work rather than the physical work. You can consider yourself as someone who is a real intellectual because of the time you invest in reading and learning.

You can be everyone's friend but not everyone can be your friend. You have a tight circle. You keep a handful of people in your inner circle to avoid drama. So to become your friend, is quite a task to be accomplished. One has to earn your trust and once they do, you become close-knit. Even so there are many levels to cross before you, the healer, call someone your close friend. After you consider someone in your group, you can even keep your life at stake for them, such is your reliability.

Likewise, your love life is quite interesting too. You exchange your soul with the one you love. Not just some superficial love affair, you tend to stay cold and temperamental in order to go through the depths of love hence you may be targeted as someone heartless in relationships. But you do not easily give in. You believe that staying in solitude and introspecting can help you choose your partner but not everyone else understands this mental state of yours. The marriage card doesn't appear unless you consider yourself worthy in terms of materialistic aspects.

You like to keep your channel of energy closed halfway. You do not like integrate with everyone you meet. You have a direct connection with the divine energies of the universe through which you heal people, figuratively. For you, the world is not what it seems to be. You delve deeper into the inner sanctum of the world to understand its meaning and its ways. You may refuse the idea of materialism and follow spirituality without giving it a second thought. Or you may enjoy every bit of what you have got, you have learnt and share it with others without any regrets.

You have no fear of being alone. Rather you love solitude. Walking in nature, petting your dog or spending time with nature and its beings is what you yearn for. Your brilliance radiates far and wide.

Negative Characteristics

How can a healer transform into someone who himself needs healing? Such is the result of the negative manifestation of the 9th Karmic number. If you are also experiencing that your divine powers have somewhat left you hollow, then you are going through the worse scenario of this number.

You start staying aloof. But this time you want to fill in the silence through random TV hopping, radio channels, excessive talking on the phone just to starve the essence of loneliness yet feel lonely inside. This is quite a difficult stage of bearing because you tend to remain confused between staying with someone or aloof owing to which the ones near you also go through the same. You may sit with your friends and family and feel flabbergasted, or you may make intimate relations with your spouse considering those acts of love as acts of vulgarity hence you start losing interest in people. You become a hermit in a sense that you become wary of everyone, you become cautious of trusting and withdraw yourself to a recluse. You need to understand that you are a worldly man. You cannot forego your duties as a family man all of a sudden. You may have faced betrayal in the past but that doesn't mean that history would keep repeating. Trust the Lord.

Lack of concern for your bodily needs and appearance clouds your judgement. You may start saving money by avoiding what is necessary to lead a normal life such as clothes, shoes or basic grooming. Even your health is put at stake by you. The only reason behind such stinginess is your dearth of self-love. You must learn to love yourself again. One heartbreak or a failure cannot limit you.

Money is a necessity with which you are familiar. However, if you still think that you can live without it, it is your error in judgement. Of whom you are jealous has understood the value of money and that is why they are earning and consuming it but it doesn't make them wrong. Going extremely ahead with intellectual and spiritual development, you may come across some theories which may not sit well together with the ways of the world. One most evident factor is the way you think of money.

You are a healer yet you have transformed yourself into a preserver for no reason. Preserving knowledge just because you deem others unworthy is called lack of compassion. The problem does not lie in you. You are a loaded barrel of knowledge. You are worthy and so is everyone else around you of learning and spitting the facts. Stop underestimating yourself and others.

Karmic Alignment

With your innate healing abilities, you may use a word and the person sitting in front of you may heal. Imagine how divinely blessed you are and then you keep everyone at bay. You are truly one of a kind.

Open yourself and your heart to others. Do not refrain from spilling the secrets of the world that you know. Make use of every moment in sharing what you have. You may have experienced pain once, twice or multiple times but that does not mean that you must recluse yourselves from others.

In loneliness you thrive. Prefer staying in nature. Go for walks. Give your undivided attention to the universe for it is the universe who has blessed you with boundless powers of healing. Writing makes you thoughtful. Put your thoughts on paper. Get rid of what disturbs you-be it logics, cautions or distrust.

Being a hermit, you are a healer. You can heal with even a word. You say the right things at right time which makes you a natural. You are a ray of hope for countless people. Your inner wisdom radiates through your words therefore choose your words carefully so you may not hurt anyone's sentiments.

Life is an opportunity to learn as many things as possible. And learning has a rule of sharing with which what you have learnt gets imprinted in your mind forever. Refrain from judging yourself and others on the basis of logics. Your logical intellectualism may deceive you from receiving the divine powers from the universe so beware.

Affirmation

I am grateful for the opportunities the universe has bestowed me with. Being a healer by nature, I can heal everyone in a jiffy. I trust myself. I love myself and the ones who love me.

10
THE WHEEL OF FORTUNE

Introduction

The idea of constant changes and evolvement is what the Karmic number 10 suggests through its wheel. Every situation has positive and negative manifestations whether one accepts or not thus the life is riding a cycle of change-ebb and flow.

The karmic code can be interpreted as the transition point in life when one has to let go off the old patterns and beliefs. One must be open to what the universe has gifted or will gift because even the problems are supposedly considered blessings in disguise because, one later on understands the importance of the obstacles in life.

Another theory which can be interpreted through the big six wheel is to become responsible of one's actions to bring the positive changes in life. It may sound simple but what you sow, so shall you reap. If one sows the positivity and positive deeds in life, the results will be the sweetest fruits.

Another factor which needs emphasis is to embrace the flow in life. One must always go with the flow to avoid any superficial difficulties. Everything is in immediate reach if one aligns himself with the universe.

Lastly, being hopeful is the essence of life. Death is not the only truth but being hopeful is another indispensable part of everyone's life who want to be in alignment with the universe.

Positive Characteristics

If someone is directly being protected by the divine powers, it becomes evident with his lifestyle and life choices. Somewhat likely is the case of the 10th Karmic Alignment number under whose influence the person gets whatever he desires in a snap, literally.

If you are that lucky person whose charts are exhibiting the big six wheel then you ought to understand the deeper levels of the quote 'Go with the flow'. Once you are able to understand that what it means, your life will be a fantasy. Whatever you shall desire for will be yours within moments. This practice does not remain restricted to the materialistic aspects but goes up till the spiritual conquests. It seems like the divine, the universe has a direct communication with you. As in when one goes to a hotel and orders what is to be eaten and within minutes everything is on the table-likewise you and your life happens to be on the same tangent. You simply decide what you want and voila! You get it.

You will always be at the right spot, doing the right thing at the right time. When it comes to relationships, what you wish for is delivered to you. Career opportunities, promotions, and new ventures-name it and you shall have it. Call it serendipity or the big six wheel showering favours on you, you must call yourself lucky during this period.

However, once you start going against the flow, the tides change, the tables turn and your life takes a dive to the rock bottom. Life stops communicating with you. The universe does not align with what you think and gives the opposite. You happen to be at the wrong place or meet the wrong sect of people. Life becomes a never-ending puzzle. Things go south at the professional front too. So beware of going against what the universe tells you. Obey the commands of the universe and all your desires will be fulfilled.

Fortunately enough, you do not have put in as much hard work as others because you are privileged. You can succeed while putting your mind in focus and delivering what the universe asks of you. You are the ones who follow others but become an exceptional follower doing the final touches. With your stroke of luck, your team wins, your company prospers, your business flourishes, you family stays harmoniously and you become the star follower.

This karma number indicates that your last life must have been quite difficult and full of hardships hence in this life you have been awarded with the best of everything. But you must keep in touch with the divine for it's divinely intervention. Without that prowess, your life can be dull.

You are supportive towards others even if you just talk to them. Assertively you have the gift of gab which makes you popular amongst your circle. The words which always spread your optimism are 'Things were, are and will be fine. Let be hopeful'. This makes you a hard-core optimist. Therefore even the universe abides by your words and makes everything butter-smooth in your life.

Always remember that under the dark cloud of blessings, the universe is showering the good fortunes on your demand.

Negative Characteristics

If the person with 10th Karmic Alignment number tends to walk the path of deviating from the universe, the manifestation takes a wrong turn hence everything in his life turns dark. He is stripped off his luck. With no magic in his prayers, he resorts to self-criticism and loathing. The universe does not align with this wishes therefore his life becomes full of struggles. With every footing, his problems keep on surrounding him while increasing in number. His focus from connecting with the supreme daggers and he creates an abyss for himself which allures poverty, penury, lifelessness and ungratefulness.

After going through your matrix, if you come across 10thKarma number in the negative manifestation then you are in for massive struggles. You ought to find the situation when you deviated from the path decide by the universe for you. As that situation must have turned the tides causing you to stagger. After breaking the divine connection, you must have gone awry in ways unimagined. With constant worries of the future, your paranoia takes over the essence of life. You can change it all by going with the flow. The more you worry, the less is the range of connection with the divinity.

It becomes imperative for you to trade the place of worry and tension with hopefulness and positivity to bring the days of glory back into your life. Just take a break from your thoughts. Focus on the present. Try to understand what the universe demands of you. As soon as you are ready to receive the signals from the universe, it would move the wheel of fortune to give you what you want.

Even if you are working as per the demands and commands of your leader, you will be forced to do what you never desired to. If you are a freelancer, you would not get work according to your capacity. You will be forced to stoop and even if you stoop, the life would bring yet another issue. In fact, as a subordinate, your senior can ask you to do unlawful activities further bringing a bigger of complications in your life. You must revive your connection with the universe when such situations crop up.

Nevertheless, you must not only rely on the magical wonders from the universe. If you work on your deeds positively, only then you shall receive positive results. Your passive approach towards life will take an inevitable turn. Your body would stay lethargic. Not only you will despise your own existence but also sit on the fence.

Karmic Alignment

You must trust the divinity, the universe, the Lord who has bestowed the powers to you however with your carelessness you deviated and are going through a lot of struggles. You must start meditating and hoping that the big six wheel will bring you the prosperity.

Relax when you feel that you have gone against the tide. Pray to the powers high above. Meditate. Ask for the guidance. The stream of consciousness plays an indispensable part herein. As soon as you open your heart, you will experience that the divinity has reconnected and is showing you the way. At that point of time, even if you feel that the way is not you had planned, just go with the flow. You will later on understand what happened and why did it happen.

Always follow your heart. Your intuitive powers knows no bounds so forget the logic and trust what your heart shows you. This shall help you to mitigate with the blunders of life, reconnect with the higher powers, create an individuality for you and help you in keeping faith in yourself for the tasks to be undertaken.

No matter what happens, you ought to be grateful for what you have. With gratitude in heart, you shall be able to attract what is missing while thanking for what you already have. Believe that yesterday happened for a reason, today is to be thankful for and tomorrow is going to be much better than you are anticipating. Stay in control of your thoughts.

Your lethargy will take a heavy toll on your health that is why you must bring discipline to your life. Consistency is as important as the order of plans to be followed. The plans can be related to the professional front or the personal but you must not forget that your health plays a prominent role in bringing out the best for you.

Follow your heart instead of following the lawless orders given by others. During the unaligned times, the others may try to make you their puppet, but you must remember to pray to the divinity for the right path to follow.

Affirmation

I am guided by the divine. I and the universe are alignment. I always go with the flow to get the ultimate gifts from the Universe.

11
JUSTICE

Introduction

The Karmic Alignment number 11 not only relates to the righteousness in the humanly nature but also divine law. It correlates with action and reaction, cause and effect and fairness and balance. This karmic number deals exclusively with karma-one ought to bear the consequences of the actions.

There are two pillars on which this karma number rests. One is fairness and the other is balance. The golden scales of balance personifies the principles of justice, truth and accountability. There is a need to take accountability for the actions and the choices made in the past.

One needs to be objective and impartial while making decisions for oneself and for others. If one has to take any decision, then the connection with the intuitive powers is so important because only with that divine intervention, one will be able to take decisions meant for the greater good. The combination of the planets Venus and Mars is what this karmic number suggests. The powers of Mars and the wisdom and impartial attitude of Venus is what makes this number very powerful.

This whole Karmic Alignment number revolves around truth and law and the re-establishment of the actions which are supposed to be aligned with the higher self.

Positive Characteristics

What one manifests is what one gets in life in the Karmic Alignment number 11. As easy as it sounds, this is one difficult task to do. The people with 11th Karmic number in their charts are prone to spontaneity in life. They can be the king one day and a pauper the next. With such sudden movements in finance, society and personal life, these people stay in a loop.

If you are currently under the influence of 11th Karmic Alignment number, you shall become workaholic. You must be one of those who can never sit idle even if they need rest. You are always on the go to do something. Your preference of work lies in sports and related activities. Professional sports is one good career option for you if you are in a fix to choose your career. Even during vacations, you like to keep your holidays full of activities, be it adventurous. Basically you feel that your body must work out as long as possible, even if you have to stretch it a bit.

You are a sun, radiating power all over the world. If your energies are not controlled by some notion, you might destroy not only others but also yourself. It may sound weird but it is what it is. The powers that you possess need to be compressed in certain situations. Your emotions can go haywire without control.

Even if you meet failure a hundred times, you still shall be working towards your goal to achieve it anyhow. You inspire others too with your undying determination. However you did not sign up tolerance and pressure from others in any way. You become intolerant when it comes to others putting you under severe pressure. You start despising their presence all of a sudden. You have a cheerful personality but clashes occur when others interfere in your matters. You are responsible, accountable and have an acumen for keeping the profits in check.

With innate strength, multiple talents and energies complementing those talents, you do not accept defeat. You can learn and earn at the same time. Delving deeper is not your choice of learning. You test the waters and dive deeper to get an insight. Other people generally test the deep waters first and then dive with caution but you, you do everything in a snap. You analyse whether anything will be beneficial or not.

Your quantity and quality of work never suffer. You may do more than one task at a time, but the deadlines will be met easily. You can become the real leaders as you have a great influence on people. Decision-making for you is a child's play. You never elongate this act which makes you a favourite amongst your senior and your subordinates. Your passion is exhibited without you moving a finger. Moreover, your passion is contagious. Others look up to you for motivation.

For some watching television makes them happy, for others materialistic things but for you, you rely on the nature to charge yourself. Such as you tend to bask in the sun, look at the moon, sleep under the stars, take a walk in the greenery, bathe near the waterfalls, and meditate on the hilltop. And to some extent, these factors help you govern your world.

You might give birth to a lot of children or your mainstream work would deal in relation with children. Regarding your health, you are a fitness freak. Which mental disorder or ailment can harm you? The answer is none.

Negative Characteristics

If you are one of those who feel that relaxation is not what you need but more work then you are suffering the negative manifestation of the 11th Karmic Alignment number without fail. You may feel that you are ever-active and can overdo the work you are into, but that is the way your sub-conscious mind helps you to navigate through the much-needed situations in which your attention is pertinent. You simply avoid a particular situation by overdoing something which doesn't really matter to you but is your defence mechanism.

Impatience runs in your veins. You want something, you can't wait to achieve it, quite relatable. But getting annoyed and frustrated while waiting makes you childish. In fact, while you wait, you tend to spit anger issues around by spreading negativity which in turn harms you more. You feel that you can do everything perfectly and on a faster pace than others because of which you suppress others so much that even they start believing in what you say.

You keep on complaining how shoddy and sluggish everyone around you is. You become excessively rude, aggressive and forget that at the end you too are a human.

With such destructive criticism, you start losing your near and dear ones. Now you are the ones who starts slacking-off. You become as lethargic as one can be. You forget that there are tasks which need completion. You run away from your responsibilities. You tend to become a parasite. And eventually you lose interest in everything around you. Your restlessness gives birth to distrust and additions of various kinds.

Especially the men, they become aggressive and are ready to pounce on anybody who comes their way. The women start gaining weight due to chakra dislocation.

You can heal others. You can lead others. You can do wonders. But you stop yourself from doing it all because you have blocked the divine energy channel.

Karmic Alignment

Relieving yourself off of the aggression, you can solve your problems by half. You must keep faith in yourself. Listen to your inner voice. Listen to what others want to say to you. Not everything can be achieved by mere force. Some things just need patience to win over.

One thing you must understand is that everyone is made up of different energies. Nobody is the same. Some people may work slowly but because they are detail-oriented, they tend to enjoy every bit of work they do. Some people, likes of you, tend to work faster because they focus on achieving their goals. They multi-task because they enjoy being under pressure. Or they might have extra energies to shed, like you do. Nobody is alike.

Train your mind to stay in the present moment. You may like to be fair and square but stay in the moment. Control your emotions through mindfulness. You can open up the divine channels to move the energy in you freely.

Women, especially, can put their energy into work through working out in the gym, getting massages, keeping their body and mind occupied. If you are a lady with this karmic number, you ought to change your ways of communicating. For instance, you must comply with the demands of your husband if you want your demands to be met. Refrain from taking him for granted. Do not put conditions on every task you do for him. Not everything is a trade.

Stop the blame game, openly and secretively. Tell your mind to change the focus from judging others to appreciating what you can do to help others. In order to transform your destructive behavioural outbursts into the higher ideas and goals, you ought to play seriously. Set yourself for tasks which can inspire thousands at the same time.

Make your life an example of forgiveness and acceptance. Instead of expecting others to follow your suit, you must inspire them effortlessly. Stop rushing yourselves and others. Let others do what they want, how they want. In case if you are being affected with their way of working, you can explain it all to them in a polite manner.

Leave the baggage behind. You cannot carry of baggage of your past to walk towards the future. Live in the present. Experience every moment in the present because time never stops. Sow your grains of fairness, justice, impartiality, politeness, understanding, leadership, acceptance, forgiveness everywhere you go. So that your future self shall reap the sweetest fruits because karma exists.

Fire element is your friend. So is earth. Choose these to meditate. You can sit on the grass to be mindful of your action-plans or you can place your hands near a bonfire to get the warmth and energies of fire.

All in all you must not forget to delve deeper into the spiritual realm by staying in the present.

Affirmation

I thank the universe for everything which I have. I respect everyone. I pray to lord for wisdom and love. I love myself and others as they are.

12
THE HANGED MAN

Introduction

The 12th Karmic Alignment number is directly associated with sacrifice, surrender and letting go of the things and feelings which are acting as an anchor. Another translation of this code is that the person has to go through a period of transition and transformation.

When one gets out of control, or feel trapped, one ought to sacrifice and surrender himself and his beliefs for the greater good of others. Pause once and observe the options-one must be tempting however the other one might be difficult at first but will prove to be much more beneficial for others too.

Another part of the great seeker shows that getting out of the old patterns, beliefs and habits promises a period of transformation. Letting go does not only gives clarity of thought but also helps in growing spiritually. There is a need during this period to get a hold of one's thought-processes because this period needs patience in every task undertaken. This is a sheer transitional period which thrives on contemplation and stillness. The evil thoughts of uncertainty and self-limiting beliefs make it all-the-more difficult for the inherent to flow with the natural flow of life.

The man hung upside down with lights radiating from his head indicates that there is a willingness to look at life and the worldly matters from a new perspective hence there should be the decision of surrendering to the natural flow.

There is a simple notion of being born, living in illusions or illusionary life, dying a significant death (metaphorical) and then being reborn as enlightened.

Positive Characteristics

With their out of box thinking, the people with 12th Karmic Alignment number tend to have a quaint viewpoint of the world around them. They might be called eccentric by some, others may call them peculiar however they have a heart of gold with a universal eye which makes them absolutely different from everyone else.

If you are lucky enough to have this Karmic number in your charts, then you must brim with benevolence, love, exceptional ideas and vision which hardly a handful people have in this world.

Your creative juices flow in a way which are uncontrollable when it comes to making sense of what and how you look at. You might be looking at a painting with your bunch of friends, and all of a sudden you would produce such extraordinary detail out of the painting that everyone else would take a few minutes to find and understand its meaning. If someone wants solutions to their problems in a non-conventional way, then you are their advisor. For some, you may become the black sheep rather in reality you are a dark horse. For people who call you black sheep may be unable to understand your view point because they have been treading the same path over and over so they think your eccentricities make you someone who cannot stay loyal. Nevertheless, the other set of people who may consider you a dark horse comprehend the ways you think. Either they wish to think like you or you have helped them in their lives in a way which is unforgettable for which they are grateful.

Your generosity knows no bounds. To corroborate this fact, your perception towards the world and its people is that how can you be at their service? The prime question which keeps on moving in your mind and heart is how you can provide assistance to the ones in need. If it is about money, you have a big heart. You believe in charity and are a Samaritan. If it comes to lending a shoulder, you are always at their beck and call. These days people need an attentive listener, with whom they can talk about how they feel, and you are that one person with whom one can talk freely, without being paranoid of getting judged. Your virtues lie in your ever open heart which is generous enough to be available for everyone. Make note that you care about yourself too. You help others in ways unimaginable but never at the cost of your own happiness. You know where to draw the line. This virtue makes you even more benevolent because one who can love himself dearly, how much would that person be capable of loving others.

Further, you are the light-bearer for others. With your creativity, you can change your foes (if any) into friends. You are a firm believer of a win-win situation. You would rather make others happy if you have to make a few compromises which will not hurt you or your resolve. But at other times, you feel a bit devastated if you say no to others for some task. You take it to heart considering it a mistake. You ought to understand that you cannot help everyone you come in contact with. It is practically impossible. Even with your philanthropy, you may not be able to help every needy in your country lest the world so there is no need to be guilt-ridden of a guilt which does not even exist.

With your innovative ideas and ingenious perception, you take over the projects for which someone with an average mind has to think over many times. It is not just your creative juices, but your self-discipline, perseverance, will-power and self-love which enables you to accomplish the tasks with such velocity that your seniors are forever impressed by you, whether you still work for them or not. However if you get into one practice of following a habit, you take forever to change or even agree to change. Sometimes, some habits take a toll on our happiness so it is better to let go instead of keeping them close.

There is no doubt about the fact that when you do with something that you love, attract abundance. Abundance of love, money and contentment. The universe works like our breath. Inhale and exhale and love what you have in order to attract the things you would like to have in your life.

Negative Characteristics

The Karmic Alignment number 12 in its negative manifestation takes away the crowning smile of the inherent and gives him the title of a pity prince owing to the fact that he is stripped off of his generosity and is given the robe of accepting what it is and how it is.

If you come across 12th Karmic number in its negative manifestation, then you would be sad to know that the tables turn quickly. Either you were a victim in the past life or you made victims through your deeds. Now you feel, in this birth, that you owe everyone one thing or the other. Saying no to someone is an emotion you never want to experience because you think that it is mandatory to appease others and keep them happy at the cost of your own happiness and principles.

You not only suppress your desires but also let go of your morality for the sake of keeping others happy. People start calling you a spineless coward even if you put your wishes on the back burner for their happiness. This soul-destructive path that you take gives way to a lot more problems in your life. This constant act of self-pity invites sufferings. You tend to entice more problems and problematic persons in life. With you as the submissive, guilt-ridden coward, even the ant-sized take the role of a lion and roar at you for no reason. Others may also start finding ways to infuriate you yet they know you will never lose your temper at them because you are so full of guilt that you think you are obliged for this kind of disrespect.

With ever-humiliating situations, you may cower before others. Complaining about injustice in life does not matter unless you stop that act of injustice with yourself. You adorn yourself with criticism. By the time you start complaining of the injustice and unfair treatment, you become a pity-magnet. It seems to you that if you would ever deny being rude to, you would be obliged to more insult. Everybody starts taking you for granted, sits on your shoulders, play with you and your emotions as if you are a puppet in their hands.

Owing to the constant struggles, insults and degradation, you fall in the hands of depression as you cannot find a way out of this kind of hell-hole. You expect others to appreciate you for what you do for them but that will never be the case. Does anyone ever is grateful for anything which he gets for free? Your life, because of you, becomes a joke and entertainment for others. They come to rant, to vent out their pent-up aggression and you take it all in just because you think they would be thankful to you afterwards.

As a consequence, you stop eating, sleeping, try to impress others much more than you can and you should. This is how you yourself attract more struggles in your life. This act of yours takes a toll on your health, your finances and lifestyle. Even your relationships also remain tensed. My dear, this is where the abyss of self-deprecation starts for you. It is not the fault of others at this point but yours and yours alone. You must know that nobody is going to thank you for being their rug.

Karmic Alignment

You must learn the balance between selflessness and selfishness. You can only give out to others what you are brimming with. If that's love you are full with, you shall spread love. If its regret, then regret is what you shall sprinkle. Lack of love in you can never help to make others happy. Transform the way you think of yourself as a victim. You are not a victim. Tell your sub-conscious mind that you are a human with feelings of remorse, guilt and regret but also love, acceptance and can also get offended.

If you think that the time has frozen, that you can never get out of the hell-hole created by you, then crack open the frozen state of mind. Start using the word 'no' when you feel uncomfortable while doing someone's work. When you have to supress your emotions, or when you have to compromise with your morality and individuality, it is time for you to take a stand against those corrupt notions and use the word NO.

Instead of making others happy, rather than prioritising others over yourself, it is time to spoil your mind, body and soul with abundance of happiness. You like massages, you go ahead. You love to go on sojourns-why not today itself? Go ahead and enjoy the best of everything. Learn to take the difficulties in your stride. Consider every obstacle as a blessing in disguise. Rather than bowing in front of mere humans, bow before the universe. The universe shall fill your heart with abundance.

Yoga, meditation, travelling, exploring the world is what your soul desires. So do not stop yourself for the sake of others. You can preach others, become spiritual leaders, reconnecting the souls in the most creative way. You can also become healers of mind and soul only if you open your heart to the universe.

Learn the art the forgiveness. Inculcate it in your daily practice. Teach it. Preach it. Help others without sacrificing your own happiness. Donate. Do charity. Join some NGOs. Ask worth of your work without hesitation. Give your unconditional love to your family and friends. Love your spouse as if there is no tomorrow.

Pour your heart and soul into the work that you do and you shall experience that others cannot stop appreciating and applauding you for the same.

Open your heart, soul and mind to the universe and you shall see miracles taking place before your eyes.

Affirmation

I am full of compassion and love for myself and for others. I always consider myself a priority over others. My existence attracts abundance and benevolence. I am grateful for who I am and how I am.

13
Death

Introduction

The 13th Karmic Alignment number may sound and look as if death took over however it is not the literal case. It summons the energy to embrace change while learning to trust the natural flow of life. The grim reaper indicates the death or the end of the old beliefs and habits which are no longer beneficial in the life of the inherent. Although this may take a lot of convincing, uncomfortable thoughts yet letting go off the past is as important as embracing the new beginnings. If the first step is not taken, one can never move on to the next step. Only letting go of something can pave the way for career opportunities and growth in the fields that one is hoping for.

In fact, this karmic number is also a sign of spiritual transformation. A subtle yet an inevitable one which brings the inherent to the horizon of changes leading to release of emotional baggage. Once the catharsis is done, the inherent starts feeling full of inner confidence.

Sometimes this karma may exhibit the stage of unemployment or a sudden unwanted change in job, or an unhealthy period, or also sometimes a dead relationship which needs a sense of renewal. An immediate travel urgency is also possible.

Water is the main element during this karmic number.

Positive Characteristics

Fearlessness and variety is what defines the nature of the people with the positive manifestation of the 13th Karmic Alignment number which defies everything superficial. In times of danger, these people can dodge a bullet without a sweat.

If you are intrepid enough, you may have seen the magic of 13th Karmic Number in your matrix which explains the fact that how you can take decisions in a spur of a moment while facing dangerous situations. Extreme sports and activities are your viewpoint of vacations. You push your limits when it comes to taking risks. There is a huge possibility that in your last birth, you must have died early so now you have taken birth to live your life on the edge because nothing scares you anymore. This applies to your professional as well as personal life.

You are that one person who wants a never-ending exhibition of variety. You live for the unstoppable changes in life. You never mind even if you have to change your whole narrative around it, you are ready to bring on the new things in life. Sitting still, staying stable is what you never yearn for. Everything that resonates with stability sounds like a disease to you.

While some people tend to lose their interest when stability leaves the table, you, on the other hand are more inclined towards those things which keep on changing their status. With a flow in your inquisitiveness, and a creative flair, you tend to withstand such situations in which the quick-wittedness is needed.

De-cluttering is your favourite hobby. Be it a space at your office which is nothing but just an old vision with no calibre, you are ready to pare it off. You do not battle an eyelid when you have to throw something which has not been in use for over a decade. For you, there is an expiry date of everything so you discard those objects which have outlived. Without the unnecessary things, you tend to focus on what is important.

If you enter a firm in quicksand, you come up with plans to save it. And you do it as a matter of fact. You remove what is not required. You cut off those things which are nothing but an appendage. Disintegration of the old into new is what you aim for while striving for success.

Just like you fancy the new things around you on an everyday basis, you too are quite unpredictable in nature. You may say one thing but refer to something else later and may act on something else altogether. In fact even you may find yourself in a fix as to what you had planned and what you have decided to do at last. You keep on setting new goals for yourself. You cannot be forced to follow the same monotonous routine day in day out.

Your courage and determination to learn new things can help you in setting yourself as an example of Jack of all trades. You are be able to procure information from others in time but as soon as you are done with your work, you may consider them useless. However you never ever stop honing your skills. Be it the skills to be used at your workplace or at home, you sharpen them every single day. No defeat or victory changes this routine of yours.

You welcome changes in your life. Whether it is a new job, a new house or a new career. You are the phoenix people look up to. You die many lives to be reborn as someone more spectacular than the last lived. Fearlessness is what you are known for. You do not fear to die a thousand deaths if you can enjoy every life as much as possible. With your straightforwardness in life, you may become a foe to many but even then you do not fear anyone. You are proud of who you are.

Your destiny is to be as valiant as one can be, to help people in ways unimaginable, to learn the lessons of spirituality even while sitting in the eye of the storm and letting go of what doesn't and can't serve you any longer. To some you may look pretentious but you do not compromise on your morals and principles for the sake of pleasing others.

Negative Characteristics

Although the positive manifestation of the 13th Karmic Alignment number makes one a hero for many, on the flip side, the negative manifestation takes down the crown of heroism and breaks it in ways which makes it irreparable.

Making it all sound offensive, the people with 13th Karma number in their matrix can make others feel worthless by mere few words without knowing the fact that their words make a huge impact. With inability to focus on the good side of anything and anyone, these people are prone to think the worst and get anxious. In fact, the thing they fear the most is death.

If you come under this code for certain period of time, you will observe that your life takes a toll on everything and everyone around you when this code is in its negative manifestation. You may tell others that they are wrong, no harm in doing that if it's apt, but you make it sound so obnoxious that the others gets offended and you don't even realise that you have hurt someone's feelings in the discourse of your speech.

You may remain anxious throughout this period owing to the fear of death. You are one fearless person however when it comes to the thought of death, be it yours or someone else's who is close to you, you almost lose yourself. Thus neglecting the gift and colours of life, you become obsessed with the thoughts of death. Death is certain. But the beautiful colours of life keep on changing. There is no certainty about the colours and hues of life therefore you must learn to live in the present rather than being trapped in the claws of the unknown future.

You may attract death in different ways though if you keep on thinking about it. In the process, you may lose your imminent health. Or you may neglect your abilities and strengths, put a halt in learning new skills or honing the old ones hence along with health you may lose sense of self-worth and determination. With such anxious attitude, concentrating on one aspect of life may sound preposterous to you thus you may turn into an extravagant and fussy. With no combination set for using your strengths and upholding or improving on your weaknesses, you may become unreliable for many thus losing out on your job or business. So you may find death in ways unimaginable. In fact some relationships may also end in nothing but regret for others and they may pass on you.

Relationships are a two way lane. Both the partners must contribute to it however if you fall short of compassion and love in a relationship then what is left of it. You may become self-piteous by repenting over your deeds which may lead to the end of a relationship. You tend to become obsessed with a dead relationship rather than watering the others which need your love and attention. You are undoubtedly close to your family, but if someone passes away, you forget everything else and focus on the one who is dead. With absolute compassion, you may feel aloof for a while but you must observe how other relations wither away during that time.

With some evidences, it can be said that you knew that your presence was unwanted at some point of time during your birth. If this was the case then you can face serious psychological trauma. How? You my lack determination to live life fully, or you may be reluctant in everything that you do. There is a possibility that you may also prefer to sit on the fence for all the major decisions in your life. Passivity is what something you are known for. Even the fear of change can fear you to an extent that you start staying in a shell of your own thoughts. In past life, maybe you were inflicted with a wound so deep that you passed away and the pain has been carried over to the present now.

Karmic Alignment

Decluttering the mind and body is quite important for you if you are going through the 13th Karmic Alignment number because the debris of the past can become a huge obstacle in building the new. However concentrating on one task is more important than doing many things at once.

You may have become habitual of starting many projects at the same time however concluding even a couple of them starts becoming a depressive task for you hence you should make it a habit to work on a couple of tasks at a time and bring them to completion. When you complete a task given to you, transformation occurs. With this transformation, the universe gives you much more than before and you start radiating it all. You must risk it all only when you feel it is imperative otherwise it is better to keep yourself on the move and develop yourself spiritually.

When you hit the saturation point, does that mean everything has ended for you? No, it hasn't. Destruction follows development. You just cannot make your life better without leaving a few things behind. It is the magical rebirth of which dies. Everything has to be transformed at some point hence death does not mean the end but a beginning to the next step. For a deeper understanding, you must up your game of spiritual learning. With this learning you may grow creatively. Just relax and let the natural flow take you where it is supposed to take you.

If you start practicing stoicism, then you may come across a point in life in which bliss and despair-everything would sound and feel the same. Nevertheless you can also consider which comes your way as a gift from the universe and be grateful for both the joys and sadness. In this way you shall be able to connect and retain the connection with the higher powers of the divine.

Learn to meditate. It may feel uncomfortable to sit for even 10 minutes however if you start practicing breathing exercises and meditation, you will experience that the universe is giving you infinite energy which might start radiating from your face and surroundings too. You shall glow inside out.

You must put a sharp focus on your health as well. Health is wealth. This adage suits you perfectly. Keep your body in shape. Your strength and endurance must find its right place. Your self-control and self-discipline comes into practice while putting your body to use by increasing its dexterity and stamina. Gym is not the only way you must tone your body but you can go on active vacations to keep your body afresh.

Open your heart to the infinite possibilities laid by the universe in your way. Once you start accepting the people and situations as they are, you will observe that life is not at all cruel. Learn to approbate life, love and pray as much as you can. Let go of what is bothering you. Visit and explore places during the vacations. Keep your body and mind in right shape and attitude to gather the infinite energy from the universe. Build your acumen to take decisions and be responsible for your actions. Leave the stressful thoughts behind and focus on things in hand. It will make your world much more beautiful.

Affirmation

I accept everything which comes my way. I respect the flow of nature. I am well aware that transformation leads to growth. I am thankful to the universe for blessing me with infinite possibilities in life.

14
TEMPERANCE

Introduction

High on feminine energies, the Karmic Alignment number 14 conveys the message to find moderation and balance in every aspect of life. It is a simple thought followed with difficulty. Temperance means finding equilibrium and calmness along with willingness to take far-sighted views to make decisions firmly.

Everything is supposedly to be done in a slow manner. The most important thing to be followed in this karma number is to exercise self-control and remain self-disciplined. Now the words self-control should not be confused with restricting the natural flow of life but the opposite. One must not try to control the ways the guardian angels protect. A mere human cannot pave the way all by himself even if he stays in this illusion. So it is better to experience inner peace by letting the nature take over and simply going with the flow.

Undeniably life is full of compromises, however one has to strike a balance between work-family and physical-spiritual realms. It may take a lot of endurance on the part of inherent however to keep serenity in place, one must follow this basic rule in life. Consequently, one can bring harmonious relationships into life through the help of moderation in everything.

Another most important part of this karmic number is to remain focused on the targets rather than focusing on what others do. When this karmic code, hits, one tends to lose focus, indulges in nefarious activities and may go through domestic strife hence it is better to focus on oneself and the goals set so that the inherent has a linear thought-process.

At the end, with moderation and a tight focus on goals, one can experience enjoyable times without any guilt.

Positive Characteristics

14th Karmic Alignment number deals with moderation and overall calmness in life. If you are going through the period of 14th Karma in your matrix, then you must be one of those people who have emotionally matured in terms of looking at your surroundings and people finely.

Anything which is beautiful attracts you and feeds you with its energy. Your hobbies include attending music concerts, going to the theatres, visiting museums to increase your knowledge. Apart from these, literature and media entice you in undefined terms. Through the hobbies that you have incorporated in your life, you get to learn the minutest details of a human mind and psychology thus you are able to distinguish people on the basis of their attitude, tone or even demeanour. You have an inkling towards what goes in their mind and in their life as a result you like to communicate a lot. With the deeper core of your soul, you yourself are a mystery to many.

Your creative juices never come to a halt. It is as if your life is meant for such things. Although your hobbies include creative activities nevertheless you prefer getting into a profession which serves your creative outflow just right such as singing, dancing, writing, photography etcetera. Activities as such provide your soul a nourishment which you cannot find anywhere else. Owing to the depth of your knowledge, sustaining any conversation-be it political, economic, psychological, or just a chill-pill, you are a pro. You can talk at length without getting off the point. Such are your skills.

You have a knack for learning different languages too. It may sound simple but it takes a lot of effort for others to do the same. Languages come easy to you. This is the reason you enjoy visiting and exploring different places on the face of earth. You love to delve into the aspects of history too hence it never becomes a task for you to learn about a place because you love doing it and even the language and history comes naturally to you.

You do what you love. Others may do what they love. You do not interfere with others and keep the opinions of others at bay when they tend to guide you. You follow your passion. And this habit of yours makes big money and name for you. Following the advice of others has never taken you far before so now you have made peace with it. You follow your heart and let it take you where it wants.

While you may stay stranded from others, but you give in emotionally. More than you, other people tend to confide their feelings in you and they feel relieved because you are such a patient listener. You radiate the feelings of support and understanding thus people gravitate towards you.

With a mature soul, you know the art of healing yourself and others through psychological help as well as herbal therapies. It may sound preposterous now but if you observe yourself, you may find glints of previous knowledge in you of the herbs used for healing. You may even find yourself inclining towards natural therapies for relaxation and freeing others of any disease. To you, inner world matters more than the outer. Be it in terms of health, beauty or work. In fact you like to judge others on the basis of their soulful talk rather than their material accomplishments. A wrong choice of word or phrase used by others can make you stay away from that person for days, weeks or even months.

Fasting, prayers, purifications-these are tools which help you to regain your lost divinity. Your healing element is water thus water is what cleanses you and your soul. Although you can become a great leader however you never strive to become one. You go with the flow. The universe guides you.

Negative Characteristics

In the negative manifestation of the 14th Karmic Alignment number, the person gets offended easily. Their mind and soul work in different directions thus the flow of creativity gets blocked. The divinity halts its supply of everything beautiful in their lives. Thus a sense of urgency makes a huge hole in their soul thus making them heartless for what they desire.

Defying the logics and reasoning, you can become a child with severe anger issues if you are currently going through the negative manifestation of the 14th Karmic number. You want everything right there and then- professionally or personally. You start to blame others in case your desires do not get fulfilled which is definitely a sign of an immature soul who has lost his spiritual practices.

Lacking the spirit of trusting the God, you rely on materialistic things thus taking you nowhere. You may trust what others say; putting faith in your own intuition is what you find dearth in. Your soulful attitude is blurred by the blockage of your divine powers.

With such heavy blockage of your divine powers, you tend to become addicted to and may indulge in matters which demand more aggression. Over-eating and going on a diet suddenly, you become unpredictable in every way possible. Basically the moderation takes a turn to South leaving behind nothing but destruction.

Karmic Alignment

Re-establish your connection with your soul. Let the universe guide you for enough damage has been made already. Bring the essence of flexible bearing in you. By all means, moderation has to be brought in by you in everything that you do and think.

Keep control of your emotions. Logic and reasoning must be brought into action before your nagging. Forget that others are obliged to serve you. You must choose your ways and order of life. Contemplate what brings you pleasure, what helps to regain your creative flow. Consider it done by the universe.

Aligning with the universe is as indispensable for you as a sailor to a ship. Meditate as often and as longer as you can. You did it all and now you have to do it all again to regain your intuitive powers. Since water is your element, prefer doing hydrotherapy as often as possible. This may cleanse you off of your sins, your negative toxins, your addictions and your revenges.

Forgiving is the path to spirituality. Learn to forgive. Nourish yourself with nature's best gifts-greenery, waterfalls, places which are waiting to be explored by you. Do what you do best-heal yourself and others too. Keep your body active. More active than ever before to bring those virtues which were in the palm of your hand during the period of positive manifestation.

Creativity knows no age, no bounds. Dive into your creative pool of activities. Do what you can to get in alignment with your soul.

Affirmation

The universe guides my soul hence my soul guides me. I am brimming with vitality, creativity and healing powers. I am in control of my senses.

15

THE DEVIL

Introduction

The 15th Karmic Alignment number may be considered mystical as compared to all the other karmic numbers owing to its name, the extraordinary, however that is not really the case because this number is directly related to the inner demons everyone has along with those unhealthy patterns or habits which let these demons gain power and rule over the inherent.

Firstly, this karmic number is in direct relation with how one feels restrained and helpless in every dark situation of his life. This is quite common yet hardly anyone expresses this form of problem. How does one feel helpless? By limiting their beliefs in themselves. One must understand that this karmic number teaches that YOU are the creator of your own destiny, let no one and nothing else rule you. There is nothing that can stop you from achieving those goals you have set however this is not the right time as the devil is setting illusionary traps hence every step which is to be taken should be cautionary because danger lies ahead.

This is the time of spiritual urgency to be led to spiritual awakening. The two figures in the karmic number refers to the temptations and desires. These material generative senses bring all the attention to themselves therefore it becomes evident that what one thinks is much more important and reliable than the actual plan set by the higher powers however this is not the suit to be followed.

The extraordinary devil encourages to experience low self-esteem, to doubt one's actions, to take revenge on others, to exhibit immense pride and be ignorant of the worldly good however this is the right time to use the self-reflection tool for personal growth. One must grow out of the illusionary traps set by the devil himself. One must resolve to face the challenges head on.

Positive Characteristics

Brimming with opportunities and a unique vision, the people going through the period of 15th Karmic Alignment number are synonymous with an X-ray machine for their observational skills. The extra-sensory abilities help them to navigate through the people.

If you are one of those who by any chance come under the influence of the positive manifestation of the 15th Karmic Alignment number, then you already know how well you tend to judge people and their abilities. You find the weaknesses which you can use to manipulate them in ways they wouldn't have expected. You, sometimes, also let others know well that how understated their abilities are and give them a heads up with their vices too.

You play some notes and people start showing the best and worst sides openly. Such as you may provoke a person to an extent that their greed and lust reveals in the worst way possible. On the other hand, you may also bring out the hidden virtues in a person when you bring him under pressure. Creativity, acumen, dedication to a project and also the will-power to face the obstacles are some of the many qualities that people show you unintentionally. There may be a chance that they themselves are unaware of these virtues in them.

One thing which you ensure that everybody around you knows is that you cannot be tricked with etiquette, manners, or lifestyle. Neither manipulation nor diplomacy works with you. One has to be straightforward in order to get your support, as simple as that. You despise pretentiousness. Owing to this quality, you find the weak links and let them go because the weaker someone is, the less time he/she will get to retain the success they have achieved. Basically, out of many ways possible you tend to test the strengths and weaknesses in everyone around you to find whether they shall excel the life tests or not.

Therefore, you are unable to retain any sort of relationships for a long time because you are habitual of testing others and not everybody is ready to prove themselves to you. They find it useless and honestly, in close relationships, if one has to prove himself/herself time and again then what is the whole point?

Physically as well as mentally you are strong enough to scare off the weaklings. However people keep on getting attracted to you no matter even if you keep testing them. People who actually want to succeed in life, they become your disciples. You leave no stone unturned in finding ways to improve someone's abilities. You prove that anybody can do anything with their strength, will-power and determination. You never ever intentionally hurt anyone however novices may get hurt. You are the one who is ready to offer his shoulder in testing times.

You are an ideal to some, a villain to others and an enigma for some. You just know whom to show your which side. And that is extremely impressive. You have intuitive powers. For some you are kind of a clairvoyant too. This is definitely something which can put an indelible mark on some people's psyche. You know how to attract money in your life.

You are the perfect combination any human wants on the face of the earth. You have a charming personality, impeccable etiquette and an attitude to sweep your seniors off the floor. No matter what the occasion is, you are always found to be well-dressed (always), and have a way with money. You are just lucky with whatever you do. You gamble as if there's no tomorrow and miraculously you always win. Always. As it has been aforementioned, you are a fantasy and an enigma too.

You are adept in adapting like a chameleon. Not only the money is dear to you but anything which you consider as yours, you never give it back. You cherish every moment with it. Loving and compassionate soul, you are one of those who accepts imperfections and still love unconditionally unlike others.

You can consider yourself an amalgamation of being materialistic as well as spiritual. You are able to manifest the perfections owing to your time and perseverance devoted to your soul therefore the universe ensures that the easy path is paved for you no matter how grim the circumstances may look.

Negative Characteristics

Once the perfect manifestation of the 15th Karmic Alignment number gets gripped by the negative influences of life, then it is doomed to be the worst example. These people fall into the trap of earthly elements which benefits no one. Indulgences, addiction, revenge and jealousy clouds their mental abilities.

When such elements gather together, another vice crops up its deadly head-aggression. Aggression against whomever you can exhibit-be it yourself in general, your family, your friends, your colleagues, your subordinates. You forget the limits while being aggressive. Inside of your mind, you think that others should be grateful to you that you are not being violent with them however you forget that your aggression is a form of violence. Violence is the weapon of the weak. Hence when you and your indulgences cannot find a way out, you become aggressive and show your colours which are ruthless.

Your jealousy loses the momentum, you become greedy as if there's no tomorrow, your mind adapts to obsession, your vanity is on its pinnacle and your indulgences-ask your close ones about how you act and react.

Your ruthlessness and addiction makes your life living hell. Try connecting to the higher powers for this is not what you are meant to be.

Karmic Alignment

You might call yourself as the saviour as you call out the vices in others however you must also take a look at yourself. Without minting words, can you become less aggressive or let go of your anger easily? There are times when people get angry, they lose their temper however that does not mean you get an excuse to become violent and aggressive. You must learn to forgive others and yourself. Stop the self -pity act. Bring a tinge of flexibility in your nature and voila! You will see that just a tinge can rock n roll your life and bring you back to who you actually are-a preacher.

In this contemporary era, everyone has some sort of addiction, be it drugs, illicit sex, or even screen addiction but you must know when to stop. Being indulgent in anything-be it even work-one can never get out of it unscathed. You ought to understand the difference between fun and being addicted. Let go of the after-effects that you experience. Replace your addictions with something powerful such as yoga, stretching, meditation or any creative outflow.

Help the weakling instead of becoming one. You have been blessed with infinite powers. You are a clairvoyant. You are an empath. Yet you behave as if you need someone to rely on. You must not forget that if you love someone, they shall love you much more. You are loved. You just need to open your heart to others. You need to change the tangent around which you think. There are positive things around you.

If there are people who do not work according to your desires, then you must find a cohesive way to tell them about it and not just toy with them. You are not God that you can test anyone. You are here to help others and not judge them.

Optimism is the key to gain divinity. You are already brimming with the divine powers within you. Why don't you help others find their strengths and keep yourself engaged with the work of the God? You shall keep receiving the love from the universe in ways unimaginable.

Affirmation

I am blessed with abilities to help others without letting them know. The universe trusts me with its divine powers. I must focus on what is good for me and for the ones around me. I am thankful to Lord for making me a calm, cooperative and understanding.

16
THE TOWER

Introduction

The Karmic Alignment number 16 may represent destruction in the first glance nevertheless it may also exhibit the first rays of sunshine after the dark night. Isn't that vaguely relatable? When one is renovating a house, one must destroy some parts of it to bring out the new structure. Likewise, one has to go through a period of destruction to bring out the most illuminating parts on the outside. This kind of destruction is a pertinent step towards growth. Not only growth but the revelation of awakening to the clarity of mind too.

It also suggests that the inherent might go through some sudden upheaval or change to bring right about the major changes on the last corner of the steep end. Although this transformation period may seem never to end nevertheless it is an uncomfortable step necessarily to be taken for a brighter future.

While sitting in the eye of the storm if one understands that this chaos is trying to change all the good to bad then it becomes an opportunity of growth rather than a milestone of destruction.

According to this karmic number, one must always be open to new ideas and perceptions about life. Life is a continuous process revolving around changes. Hence be ready to let go off the old for the sake of new. If taken from a bird's eye view, every wreck is followed by creation therefore big changes always take place after one accepts that changes are much-needed.

Positive Characteristics

When one has cleared the levels of the game set by God, muddled through the emotional turmoil, has met and fought with countless earthly temptations, there comes a time when he is ready for the transformation. Call it an awakening or just a simple transition but it creates an earth-shattering reality. This reality check entails the most important information from the God himself- stay in the present, focus on the present, live for and in the present. Isn't that simple to understand? No. It is not for most of the people living on the face of earth however this is the motto the person under the influence of the 16th Karmic Alignment number to live for.

If you too are currently in the influence of the positive manifestation of the Karmic Number 16, then you are a unique personality with a unique vision and transformative energies. By staying in the present moment, you are able to look at the world with a new perspective of joy and vitality thus you tend to incorporate more conscious and spiritual approach. By changing the way you think, you have already accepted the things as they are and that is, my friend, a good start.

To be spiritually awakened is one thing but you are into transformation too. While spiritual awakening doesn't happen over a day, it goes a long way and it helps to encapsulate life's priorities. The transformation on the other way is all about storm first rain later kind of thing. For transforming oneself, a person needs a lot of energy-both mental and physical. You are ready to bring changes in your life, in all aspects. You are ready to let go off the stagnancy of life, the stability, the earthly temptations, the attachments and the dependencies to receive much more from the universe. You are ready to face the challenges heads on with anything that comes to oppose you or test you in the process of transformation.

You are the light bearer and the path paver for many in your life. With extremities of physical and spiritual energies, you become ruthless at times but your heart knows no bounds when it comes to kindness.

You learn. You learn a lot. You learn from different sources but spread the knowledge as one. You are a seeker of wisdom, knowledge and spirituality.

You like to teach others what you have learnt because only then you feel that you have learnt something.

With your eccentric ways of thinking and coming up with solutions, you become the leader. You think out of the box owing to which you are a go-to for every person in your office and family. Innovation and creativity are always on the tip of your tongue. Somewhat you have a direct connection with the people in the positive manifestation of the 15th Karmic number.

You make palaces out of mere dirt. You have psychological and spiritual powers which help you to transform rubble into magnificence. The ruins of an obsolete world can be converted into a prosperous one if you put your energies into it. Once you do, there is no going back. You become the alpha. You cross hurdles as if they are child's play.

With sheer determination, you tend to be decisive in moments of stagnation. It seems to you that stagnation is a deadly virus which if gets in touch with you, your capabilities shall vanish all of a sudden. You like the situations to develop. Stability is an old concept for you. You like stability as long as your plans are developing. As soon as you think that it is time for development, you throw away the concept of stability to the dogs and risk everything you got just to develop. Your development strategies are infectious. Anybody who comes in contact with your plans of development, he gets influenced without even trying.

Negative Characteristics

If you are under the Karmic Alignment number 16, you may have experienced or are yet to experience sudden health problems, accidents quite often and also poor mental conditions.

Since you have already decided to let go off the earthly attachments and decided to spiritually awaken your soul; wailing for materialistic pleasures will be of no use because the universe has decided your fate now. You just can't back out.

You may think that you can keep violating the rules of the land where you live however it is not the case. You may be summoned by the higher powers in ways which are beyond your imagination. Destruction at every possible step, staggering life-you may face the consequences of the deeds you have undergone in the worst way possible.

Imposing your will on others or getting aggressive when others do not understand what you intend to say are major flaws in you. Dominating attitude is what you are notorious for in your friends and family.

Basically you are left with two choices-one is to awaken spiritually or become the reason for your own destruction. None is easy. But bearing the repercussions of the latter is a tough job which will ultimately result in the former option. Since you are already a tough nut to crack, you may find solace in knowing that if you ever back down, you will end up having a glorious future.

Karmic Alignment

This is the moment when you must stay in the present, pray to God for wisdom, strength, rethink your morals and principles and change your perspective of the world. Change your ways of viewing others. Lose your aggression and your vanity.

You should master the world of matter since you are born in this world yet getting attached to them is not really an option for you. Live in the present. Relax! Nobody is going to cut off your legs if you don't participate in the activities the average humans enjoy. You are a God's being. Act like one.

Mindfulness should become an indispensable part of your life. De-clutter your mind from the toxic thoughts, negativity and earthly attachments. You have a knack to learn and teach spirituality hence do what you have been sent to do. Give your house a much-needed cleanse. Even your body and mind have been longing for cleanse since forever. Strengthen body, mind and soul after cleansing. Eventually these are going to be your best friends.

Open your heart. Let go of what scares you. Ascend the steps towards humility and kindness. You may already be an example of success after failures to many. Epitomise benevolence and spiritual knowledge.

Start meditating. This will transform your mental and nervous breakdown into a spectacular view. Nothing happens by chance. The energies vested in you are given directly through the channel of divinity. You just need to be receptive to the natural flow of the universe. You will come across the signs yourself, effortlessly. You are always enveloped by the higher powers.

Expand your horizons of learning and success. Be open to changes. Let go of what hurts you rather drip with divinity.

Affirmation

The universe has trust in me and my abilities. I shall learn and preach spirituality. No earthly indulgences can break my focus set on the spiritual awakening. I am proud of who I am.

17
THE STAR

Introduction

The Karmic Alignment number 17 symbolises that even in the darkest time, there is hope and a new beginning on the horizon. Henceforth, this karmic number helps one to navigate through the destructive times. With faith in the future, hope healing the mind and body, and a constant feeling of renewal and inspiration, one can gather the courage to move through the wreckage with a strong heart, unwavering and unfalteringly.

No matter what the circumstances are, the connection the divine is always present however in the times of this karma, one experiences that the divine connection is stronger than ever before. There is a renewed sense of purpose in what the inherent does and wants. Moreover with such spiritual awakening and awareness of this awakening, new beginnings start taking place, the inherent, effortlessly, starts walking on the right path as a consequence he relieves himself of all the guilt and remorse he ever felt and finally achieves his goals and targets set by him.

The confidence in the future increases manifold so does the trust in one's abilities. A sense of gratitude, a sense stating that one is truly blessed by the universe in all forms possible, can be felt by the inherent. Being a mediator of good vibes, this energy can become contagious and let others feel the same. Hence the part of healing inside and out along with healing others starts taking place.

Positive Characteristics

Anybody who is eccentric while thinking out of the box, and who can become the centre of attraction within a few minutes of entering a party- consider them a person who has the influence of the 17th Karmic Alignment number in their life.

If you are the soul of a party, if you think yourself full of creative juices and you also let them flow in ways unimaginable, then you, my friend, are under the positive manifestation of the 17th karma which is the path of renewal. The universe hears you, understands you and blesses you therefore with whatever you ask for. Since your relation with the universe is quite tight, you are considered special without any specific reason. Also, you have great vibes emanating from you. Art is your forte. You like to be appreciated on stage, you love being noticed in a crowd. You admire the spotlight you get from everyone around you.

Others love to be with you. The ones who cannot, they pray to be found in the same vicinity as you. With your good sense of humour and art of story-telling, you are good with people. While you gesticulate a lot, you also tend to be quite focused on your dress sense. You deal lovingly with people. Sometimes, you heal others with your words merely. You must consider yourself a star as you shine bright and others keep on admiring you for who you are.

Even if you are dressed simply, you emanate the vibrations of being quaint and beautiful at the same time. No matter what you choose to do, you always bring out the best in your job through your barrel full of creativity. Fame is at your disposal. With your massive sense of receptiveness and intuition, you dream vividly and think dreamily. Your feet are always up in the clouds somewhere. But you have golden hands. With your one touch, they whole city lights up. You can light up anyone's world.

With you in a business, one can never go wrong because the universe lightens your path. You are the star of your own destiny. You can make wonders in a business without even the capital investment lest a job. With your skillset, you are confident about what is supposed to be done. You can never let your voice fade away. The star is you who is always visible to others. You are made up of creativity, special talents and a touch of Godly perfection too.

Your energy captivates, enchants and bewitches others. You find your path yourself, tread it with confidence no matter how difficult it is and you come out as the winner. For others, it may be a cake walk but you know what you had to do to make it look like a cakewalk.

Nature and the things of nature are your best friends.

Negative Characteristics

Tables turn immediately for the ones who find themselves under the negative influence of the 17th Karmic Alignment number. Creativity turns into a matter of argument, the self-idolised Godly image, in which the persons start feeling comfortable while making others feel dead.

If you feel that you cannot combine your talents with the job at the given moment, because you think that creativity is but a scam which is meant to keep one poor throughout his life, then you are in here for the negative manifestation of the star which is the 17th karma. You are creative but you cannot sell your creativity-that is what makes you feel negative and full of despair, and that is how you start believing in the fact that the artists are meant to remain poor and hungry rather than accomplished.

Consequently, you start feeling like you have lost on everything. You become extinct. You feel dead and morose. You feel redundant even when happy. You stop dressing up, making people laugh at your jokes because you think of yourself many steps away from the confident self.

On the other hand, you may also feel as if the whole world is nothing but a worm to you whom you can crush in a fraction of a minute. You may start thinking of yourself as someone with high spiritual attainments and may be a part or the human form of God and start treating others full of errors. This fever of self-importance may bring you to a stage where you shall only communicate with the ones above you and shall deem others inferior. Your focus remains on the egoistic part of yours.

Thus, when everything seems overboard, pride cures you. You are left bereft of everything that you possessed before. Your image of self-importance makes you no more than a person of no value in the world.

Your circle of progression and regression cannot stop until you tame yourself, your habits, your line of though and your way of life.

Karmic Alignment

The universe is the highest power. You must remember this even if you are considered as a part of Godliness. Your creativity knows no bounds and shall also help you to earn a good sum of money only if you focus on amalgamating the two.

Your confidence is innate so is your pride yet none should overpower you. You must keep yourself grounded, no matter how high you fly. You must allow yourself to be famous rather than notorious.

Find your stellar path to success. Find your niche. Once you do, try to improve every single day. Do it because you want to not because you have to. And if you have to do it, then remember the primary reason behind the obligation. You are a divine channel of healing and creative energies. You must own it all. No matter what step you take, you are always under the divine protection. However make that protection count. Pay your debts to the universe by following the right scheme of work.

Meditation shall help you in ways unimaginable and uncountable. So would the nature. Explore the natural place. Walk with the wild, in the wild for you are a star with healing properties. Stay in positivity. Thrive in positive vibes. Strive for perfection in yourself. Break the obstacles of self-doubt and fears for you are the star of your own destiny. What you fear might be the way to success.

Learn to walk the path with one thought in mind-every failure is a blessing in disguise for you. Nobody can beat you unless you yourself do so. Keep faith in you. Keep faith in the universal powers.

Affirmation

I thrive in creativity and brim with healing powers. I do what the universe tells me to. I am grateful for being the star of my own destiny.

18
THE MOON

Introduction

The Karmic Alignment number 18 is in direct association with understanding and embracing the unknown and putting trust in one's instinct rather than on logic and reasoning solely. Although, this karma number suggests that one may feel trapped inside the abyss of anxiety owing to the power of the sub-conscious mind and the mysterious aspects of the life which are still incomprehensible to the average man, the inherent may feel as if he is engulfed by the fear of the unknown owing to which he may go through a period of emotional turmoil and uncertainty.

During this period when one may feel that the path is lost, that the life has become vague and it may seem useless, it must be understood that the time has arrived when one ought to trust his intuitive powers and inner flame to navigate. Navigation is only possible when the mind is clear, the conscience is roaring and the logics are thrown out of the window. Then only there shall be no confusion whatsoever.

One can experience that fear has overcome the faith creating illusionary tactics to leave an imprint of stress and anxiety however one must be committed to his optimism to come out of this dark illusion.

This karmic number also suggests that there are dark secrets, hidden ulterior motives and unseen deceit and manipulation taking place in the immediate surroundings one should become aware of. These may be called to explore the shadows and confront desires and the deepest fears. Hence herein the logic may not work but intuition will work wonders.

Positive Characteristics

Ever heard of someone who was afraid of the dark yet walked into the darkest alley with confidence and came out as fearless? Or someone who manifests what he wants through his dreams and communicates his thoughts through words without compromising anyone's dignity? Or have you come across a person who works like a dog in one half of the months and hibernates in the second half of the month? If the answer is yes to all of the questions above, then you must have across a person who is under the positive influence of the 18th Karmic Alignment number which is directly associated with the moon. Magic is at their core.

If you are one lucky person with the positive manifestation of this code, then you are in here for a luck pot because you actually achieve what you believe in. The law of attraction says that what one conceives, then believes is what he achieves-and this is apt for your line of thought these days. Your visual-auditory-kinaesthetic images help you explore and win the world at the same time.

Your excellence intuitive abilities aid you in becoming the white magicians. You can ask for answers from the universe and you get your answers through your dreams, isn't that so fascinating? For you, maybe a regular thing but for others it is indeed magical. The depth of your inner world knows no bounds so does your mesmerizing nature. For your contemporaries, you are a riddle with absolute enigmatic virtues.

Your cycle of life works with the lunar cycle. Full moon dictates your highest potential whereas the waning moon keeps on obliterating your prowess. If you feel morose during the period of full moon, then it is time to rethink your habits or your decisions. You simply have to rely on the moon for your life changing decisions.

Your manifesting abilities are first class. How? Because the moon is a magnet in the universe and so are you during this phase. What you think of, comes in your life without keeping you on hold. If you want something, just try this out in case you are unaware of your abilities, just concentrate on it and voila! You shall get it in a blink of an eye.

Most of your interests lie in magic, clairvoyance, telepathy, mysticism, occultism or something related to your rituals. You may become so passionate about your interests that you may choose any of those as your profession too. Since creativity of yours is flexible and non-linear, you tend to choose profession as such which can become a medium of transferring the creative juices into the work itself. The high energies help you to achieve the levels in your work which are considered next level.

You may have never been a fan of writing and telling your emotions through words but now as the moon helps you to gravitate towards art and its branches, you are inclined towards writing whatever you feel. You think that your life depends on the words you write. Your creativity feels justified when you write something on your own. You create beauty around you with the words you write.

Since the moon is protected by the water element, likewise you too are protected with water. Cleanse yourself and your energies with water. Your level of healing, purifying yourself and also helping the body to judge the levels of positivity, you must use water. Drink lots of pure Himalayan water if you can to enhance your energies. Staying in depression or near the depressive energies should not be your call. It is imperative for you to grow out of dark to achieve your levels of spirituality. As the moon in its negative influence cannot even conquer its soul lest you.

You overcome your fears. It is not possible for a human to not fear something but you always conquer your fears somehow. You are scared but still you never let your sense of awareness go awry.

Negative Characteristics

Fear, obsession, paranoia and darkness- everything related to it all and its paraphernalia are what govern the inherent who is spending his time under the negative influence of the 18th Karmic Alignment number. As simply arranged, this kind of life can become a depressive standard of living since everything in its negative connotation is devoted to the person with 18th karma.

If you too are being attracted towards the waning aspects of moon in the human form, then you are definitely going through the negative manifestation of the moon. You may or may not be attracted towards black magic but sometimes your line of thought sticks to such occultism and you feel if you can do it to gain what you want in life. You may use such tactics to achieve what and whom you want in life. You sometimes tend to forget and cross the thin line between possessiveness and obsession.

If you and someone else is not on the same page and you feel they ignite negativity in you, you become vindictive. You eye-jinx them and things start to fall apart in their lives. They become clueless to what is happening with them whereas you are quite proud yet fear the consequences of the same because you are well-aware of what you have done. Your manifestation, whether positive or negative, is reliable in all the cases hence you can use it in either way.

You become afraid of everything lively, full of light such as fire because you personify the dark moon phase in your life. You start facing paranoia of all kinds. You brim with ifs and buts. You forget that there is a perfect circle. If you haven't done anything wrong with anyone, then you mustn't be afraid.

You start imagining in ways which if get materialised in your life, you may fall apart quite too soon. You may say that you are not afraid of anything but you get scared as a wet cat in your mind. You start living in illusions created by you. And then you may start thinking that how did your life become such a mess.

For every negative thought, you must inculcate two positive thoughts in your mind. Only then your circle of darkness can end. You may also be lost in choosing your goals. In that case, your ability to shine through may vanquish. Later on these things may bring you to a closed self, a depletion of the good energy and burdensome habits. Unfortunately, depression may become your best friend too.

Karmic Alignment

Unleash your creativity. Let your creative juices flow in directions you never explored for you may later on realise that these were the right ways. Identifying your fears and conquering them can ease out a lot of things for you. Clear your mind off the negativity you have been brewing since forever. Others may never even hurt you but your wrong manifestation or perception can alter the course of their lives since you have innate ability to manifest everything accordingly.

This is the moment you live for. This is the moment you must live in. Present is the present, a gift, everyone has but hardly anybody notices this gift until the moment is lost. You have been given this magical power but you need to learn to use it for some greater purposes. Your touch of love, your love for divinity and for others can bring so much unanticipated harmony in your life as well as the lives of the others.

You ought to comprehend that what is the priority and what can be put on the back burner, even if it is for a while. Map your goals. Learn to understand what it means to set goals and achieve them. Visualize yourself as if you have already achieved these goals. Thank the universe, the divinity, for helping you in achieving your set goals.

There is one magical karmic alignment practice which you can do-you must write down your dreams, whatever you dream is a sign. Now if you start writing those daily, you will realise there is a pattern and then it will be butter-smooth for you to read the language of your dreams. In this way, your intuitive powers too will gain momentum.

Be good and do good should be the motto of your life. Undoubtedly you follow this approach but when sometimes the moon phases change your phase, then you must inculcate the practice of forcing yourself to think that karma is a real thing. Treat yourself with love and affection. Do yourself favours. Take care of your body, mind and soul and you shall reach the heavenly places.

On the full moon nights, you must perform rituals. Pray for unconditional love, prosperity, harmony and all the good things for yourself and your family along with the rest of the world and in no time you will see how the world has turned into a heaven for you.

Refrain from drawing conclusions on the basis of your knowledge. You may know a lot of things but not everything. Illusion is completely different from reality.

Affirmation

I manifest all the good things. A grateful being, I am who I am because of the divine powers given by the universe. I always focus on the positive.

19
THE SUN

Introduction

The auspicious Karmic Alignment number 19th is synonymous with vitality and happiness. The radiant sun is a symbol of hope, renewal, growth and enlightenment hence this karma number promises a lot of positivity and success.

The sun issues a warrant of clarity to those who have been living in the dark. It is time to come out of the illusions and face the daring sense of purpose. No more hiding behind the excuses will give rise to the opportunities at work and in personal life. If one sets afoot in the warmth and light of the sun, he shall experience bliss and love. Apart from these, one may also undergo a deep sense of connection with the self, which is the greater purpose of life on earth. The radiance may also symbolise a lot of initiatives to be taken, fame and name to be achieved and targets to be met. With childlike innocence one may experience bliss but with such creativity and vitality, one is sure to hack the pinnacles of success.

During this karmic period, the relationships flourish, growth and expansion knows no bounds, and radiant health and vitality gives way to wisdom and clarity of mind thus promising positive outcomes in all spheres of life.

Positive Characteristics

Being the centre of the universe, with enormous light radiating from it, the sun is supposed to be the fire ball which keeps every other planet in order. Likewise, a person under the positive influence of the 19th Karmic Alignment number.

If you, with your powerful effulgence, come under the category of the Karmic number 19, then you must be a cynosure unwantedly. You must be the philanthropist of your own world. Your energy potential, your creative juices are for the world to explore but for you it's a given. You are extremely open when it comes to giving others what you have-abundance. Owing to this fact, many people hover around you like bees.

Being a hard-core optimist, you like to keep others happy around you. You are a giver. You tend to engage yourself in public activities, charity functions and alike. You may find yourself a good arena for work however any area of work you choose, you shall shine bright like the sun. You are a leader, no doubt, but it takes a lot to be a leader. Miraculously, it doesn't tire you but adversely makes you much more efficient. You tend to manage time with such perfection that you not only balance work and personal life but also are able to get some time-out for philanthropy, over-the-top tasks.

You are materialistic but you ought to understand that your karma resonates with spirituality rather than materialism. If you work against the clock to help others in their testing times, then you shall realise that money is the by-product but the main essence is kindness and spiritual satisfaction for which you live. If you are able to accomplish the deeds for the greater good, you shall get the material satisfaction too along with spiritual awakening. Your love language, unlike others, is service. You like to host family dinners, parties, get-togethers and the like for your family and friends. Sometimes organising meals for complete strangers may sound normal to you. You do it on daily basis without fail.

Just like the radiant sun, your personality cannot stay hidden for a long time. Your love for others, your acts of service, your leadership qualities are a sum of your whole which are transparent even in situations when you feel like staying behind the curtains. Unwantedly you get attention from everyone. You rarely fall in the trap of depression and anxiety. But if you are bereft of your creativity and action-mode, you may feel morose.

With your virtues, you feel everybody is destined for one thing or the other hence you do not understand why people face difficulties. You believe everyone has talent of some kind. So why don't they use it all for their own benefit. Looking at people living a lifeless life makes you sad. You have an innate quality of being an empath.

Your life goals are different from rest of the population. Spreading warmth and knowledge is your foremost task. Radiating every nook and corner of your surroundings with light of wisdom and kindness is what you have been sent to earth for. Moreover, love, beauty and joy are all you are filled with. Thus your tasks must be taken as global tasks. However, just like the sun, your warmth should go everywhere rather than focusing on one person or one aspect of life. For instance, if you focus your love, joy, warmth, healing energies on just one person, then it might backfire harder than you ever thought it would. Even the person getting your energies would also feel the pain and despair.

Your energies need dynamism. You need variety. If you do not get the variations in life, you feel unaccomplished and start to shed your responsibilities. For this you must participate in social activities where your focus can be deviated to various activities. You are one of those optimistic people who are the life, body and soul of a party, a place or an occasion so do not lose your element.

Negative Characteristics

If the rays of the sun can radiate every nook and corner, it also can extinguish the lives off from the face of earth. With its authority and vanity, it can turn everything into ash. Thus the negative manifestation of the sun is as merciless as its rays.

Now if I may, do you feel that people owe you respect? Do you consider others' viewpoint as nothing less than cacophony? Do you believe that you should become the leader everywhere whether your qualities are connected to the work or not? Do you think money is everything and the rest is nothing more than a piece of waste? If your answers are yes in a row, mind you, you are under the negative manifestation of the 19th Karmic Alignment number which can make you feel devoid of authority, control and satisfaction of any kind.

Basically, the problem arises when you feel that everyone owes you respect irrespective of your deeds. Your obsession of being the cynosure is something you can't shake off. Thus the vice of vanity births many more vices. You want everyone to follow your lead, abide by your rules and just keep on listening to you while you banter about how everything should be. Isn't that unfair to others? Your viewpoint ought to be corroborated by others. If anyone fails to incorporate your principles and linear thinking into lives, then they are obliged to face your rudest behaviour.

If you may notice, people would start running away from you. Your overly authoritative attitude would scare them off. This may lead to gap in communications and while you may think that others are underperforming, you will realise at some point that it was all about misdirection of your thoughts.

You can become quite interfering in the lives of your close ones. You become the peeping Tom. Your nose enters into others' business which can create a horrid atmosphere. Take a break! Let loose! You cannot and should not control everyone. It is practically impossible. Uninvited suggestions are never welcomed-you must engrave it in your mind.

Utterly poor, absolute penury is what defines the negative connotation of the radiant sun.

Karmic Alignment

Find a job which helps you to pique your interest. Get a hobby which can help you eliminate the self-obsession of being perfect. Refrain from living for others. Live for yourself because at the end of the day, what you think and feel is much more important than others' viewpoint. Work on your appearance. Strive to improve yourself rather than forcing others to improve. Become an example rather than an effigy to be burnt.

You have indubitably, abundance of knowledge and love to spread and share. Your creative juices need a muse. Work on yourself and your sense of aggression and guilt. You shall realise that everyone, including you, have a couple of flaws but these must not be exaggerated to make others feel bad about themselves.

Distribute your energy rather than dumping it. The sun is the leader who never differentiates between anyone. Become the sun. With your radiant personality, immense knowledge and positive vibes, you can earn money as if it's a cakewalk if you work on your appearance. Start a fitness regime. Doesn't matter what your gender is, what matters the most is the way you execute your physical traits.

Develop spirituality and conquer the demon of inner aggression. With spirituality, your mind will tap into your hidden potential. Engaging in the social projects can help you devour your sense of guilt in many ways. With your natural healing abilities and warmth of love and joy, you can make anyone's life full of happiness and prosperity.

Never forget that what you give to the universe, the results you get are manifold of what you gave. Thus if you start donating even a 10% of your earnings, you may realise soon enough that your earnings have increased by manifold. You should epitomise the light, the radiance, the love, the knowledge and the liveliness.

Refrain from resenting yourself or others. You may never grow out of resentment. It is meant for the losers. And you my friend are born to be a winner. Let go of what happened in the past and ensure that your present is respected by you, as a consequence your future will be secure. You are the sun and it is your responsibility to be an example of perfection in discipline yet while being flexible.

Affirmation

I epitomise the warmth, the joy, the wisdom of the sun. I am a being with flexible yet disciplined outlook who lets the creative juices flow in order to help others and myself.

20
JUDGEMENT

Introduction

A path of awakening, renewal and transition is what the 20th Karmic Alignment number suggests. When one reaches a crossroad wherein a single path has to be chosen, this Karmic number plays a vital role.

The awakening symbolises the recalling to the past actions for which the inherent must take responsibility to bear the consequences. There are three personifications in this instance. The first being forgiveness, the second is redemption and the third one is the way to the 2nd chance.

This Karmic Code also represents the transformation of the inherent. In simple terms, it is a sign to let go off of the old patterns and habits while embracing and inculcating the new ones to enjoy the brick-load of opportunities and changes better than before.

Based on the inner truths and values, one is called for a spiritual awakening or a higher purpose here on the face of the earth.

Positive Characteristics

Ever heard of someone who have had premonition about what will happen next? Or anyone who is able to talk to their ancestry through dreams? If you are the lucky person going through the same phenomenal time, then you are under the positive influence of the 20th Karmic Alignment number which is judgement. As the name suggests, the inherent is able to judge what will happen next and what has happened in the past.

You have an unbeatable relation with your ancestors. Your intuitive powers know no bounds when it comes to retaining important information. You speak out the ideas as if you are kid in whose ears someone has whispered the right answers. Déjà vu is your best friend. Like every human, you have lived many lives but the strange part herein is that you might remember many of them if you put your mind on it. Additionally, your supersonic power is to help others in deriving the solution to their problems through the help of your intuitive ability and premonitions.

Do not take your dreams for granted as your ancestors are showing you the ways to deal with obstacles in your life. You may wake up and be ready to work on an idea about which you had never thought of before. At times, you might be astonished at your ability to execute difficult projects when in the first place you had not even thought about treading that path.

Spiritual awakening is at your core. You tend to help others through your dreams, make their life goals seem easy with your strategic planning. Not only your colleagues or subordinates but your family also gains a lot from your exceptional virtues. You solve the problems left in between by your ancestors as if it's a child's play. In fact, your ancestors return the favour by letting you know what will happen next in your life as well as your family's life. The ancestors help you even in deciding what you should do and what should you ignore or refrain from.

You love your family. You love your roots, your history. You may feel a special connection with your ancestors. Any long-lost relative do not go empty-handed from your house lest the close ones. Such is your relationship with your family, both maternal and paternal that you epitomise the love.

You are exceptionally close to your ancestors however that does not mean that you should follow their footsteps as you may also end up like them, relying on your progeny for salvation of your karmas. Since your time is to be spent in laying off what they did, you must tread your own path. As a result, there is a chance that death may not frighten you as much as it frightens others. You already have comprehended the philosophy of life and death hence you are not afraid of what lays ahead.

With your extra-sensory abilities, you are able to learn what is supposed to happen in the future, be it occupational projects or hazards, hobbies to be cropped yet in the contemporary or what is yet to be revealed to the world. You are attracted towards the unknown and the unusual without an anchor. You love to study and incorporate laws of the universe and heavenly guidance in your life.

You must not forget the main karma of yours which is to finish what you couldn't in your past lives.

Negative Characteristics

Do you believe in parenting? Have you started despising your parents? If something is wrong in your life, then do you play the blame-game with your parents? Has your ancestral wealth not been up to the mark? You feel me? Yeah, then you are definitely under the negative influence of the 20th karmic alignment number. Your problem starts and ends with blaming your relationship with your family.

You just cannot accept your maternal or your paternal family as they are. You consider them snakes. According to you, everything that has gone wrong in your life is because of the kind of relatives you have. It is their fault. Judging others and giving birth to conflicts is your new hobby because you are short on money as you cannot focus well on your occupation, however that is not your fault, right?

Teaching your parents the basics of life and humiliating them is the sole reason you wake up every morning. You know the world much better than them, isn't it? Why are you living in such illusion? You can be more educated than your parents, thanks to them for that, however you can never be more experienced and wise than them but you think that you are. That is why the resentment accumulates into a fireball which burns you and your relationships.

With everything going in a circle, it creates vicious atmosphere for you everywhere. You cannot focus on the karmic tasks assigned to you. Your parents are not at fault for what is happening in your life. You must become accountable enough to own your mistakes and move on to focus on for what you have been sent here on earth.

Karmic Alignment

Refrain yourself from the blame-game you play with your parents. Your parents brought you here, now it is your turn to build your karma. In your case, you have been given another chance to recuperate for what you lost in the past lives, to compensate for yourself and your ancestors. Forgiveness and acceptance are the two anecdotes which you must imply with at all times during this dark negative period of your life.

Miraculously, you have psychic abilities. Why not find the purpose for them rather than spreading hate, right? Elevate your thoughts. And you may find yourself united with the higher powers once again. Pray and meditate. Replace inner aggression with inner peace. Let go of what happened in the past. You cannot change it but you can definitely transform your future by being in the present and flowing as your karma guides you to.

It is sheer luck that you have been chosen in this family out of the whole ancestral roots. Don't you find it comforting to know that your parents desired for you and that is why you are here? Isn't it possible that you might not have been the right kind of parent to your children in the past lives, and that is why you think that your parents are not who you need?

Let go of the judgements you make about others, let go of the mistakes. Learn to forgive and forget. Nobody apart from you is being cruel to you. Be yourself in the best possible way. Learn to serve your intuition. Once you start doing all that you have been asked to, you will notice massive changes in your surroundings. You shall even become a great example of a perfect son/daughter to your children. You may lead them towards the right path.

Affirmation

I am the stream of consciousness between my ancestors and my progeny. I forgive and forget to move on to higher plateaus in life. I am grateful for who I am and who shall I become.

21

THE WORLD

Introduction

The Karmic Alignment number 21 is often seen as the symbol of completion, fulfilment and achievement. The wreath represents the infinite cycles of birth, death and rebirth. It also represents the attainment of the long-term goals or the successful execution of a major project.

This Karmic number exhibits the fact that the inherent has reached the saturation point of success, a milestone which was thought to be a distant dream. And is now on board with the idea of moving forward. The wholeness and integration found through this Karma number is quite fulfilling as it shows that the sense of balance and harmony have been achieved.

In other terms, this Karmic Alignment number shows the relation between the inherent and the universe, achieving the connection to the highest spiritual purpose. A sign of encouragement and evolvement is evident in the 21st Karma.

Positive Characteristics

With greater good in their minds, these peacemakers value the world as it is when the karmic alignment number 21 is in the positive manifestation. If you feel confident in achieving your goals and love to meditate alongside then you are under the influence of the Completion.

Naturally gifted with an innate sense of connection with existence, you are healers with proficient healing properties. With your peace-making attitude, conflicts stay at bay. Consider yourself as someone who can sacrifice their own happiness for the sake of the greater good. With boundless love and hope, you keep faith in the universe and its powers in helping you set and achieve the goals.

With a cosmopolitan soul, you love to explore different ethnicities, cultures and their traditions. You have a knack of travelling, being friendly at the most hostile places and leaving behind your trail of happiness on the way forward. Learning foreign languages is a cakewalk for you. Since you travel around a lot, your profession somehow matches your passion for globetrotting. You are absolutely adept in adapting as per the conditions required.

By moving so much around, your ambitions increase so does your ability to deal with difficult situations. You draw inspiration from the worldly places hence you become one of a kind in many aspects. With your enormous will-power and strength, you combat with the most dangerous in a wishful manner thus resolving the matters quickly. You attach yourself to those who are kind and who spread peace.

You can also choose to become a psychologist or a counsellor who can in some way or the other help people in leading the desired lives. Meditation is the keynote of your life. You must keep on meditating as long as you can to achieve your goals.

A romantic jargon: you may meet your soul-mate on one of the foreign trips you go to. It will change your destiny in much better way.

Negative Characteristics

What an absolute transformation of line of thought! The so-called peacemaker turns into an instigator. During this timeline, if you are under the negative influence of the 21st karmic alignment number, then you are bound to have animalistic feelings for the whole world around you, whether they hurt you or not. You create an atmosphere of animosity everywhere you go.

Your aggression leaves the limit at the doorstep. With full throttle, you pounce on people who go against your tide. Initiating a war, a conflict, global cataclysms phobia, and maybe isolation from the whole world become your favourites. You limit yourself in every way possible.

However, you tend to forget your limits at pursuing for loans. You can and must take a loan if needed for work and business otherwise any loan taken for the sake of your desires and passions may result in nothing but a canyon-ball.

Giving yourself the advice, the healing in somewhat different ways is totally prohibited for you. Do not become your own doctor. The world is not as dangerous as you think it is. The doctors will not kill you. So stop judging them. Even your resilience and patience can bring the right amount of happiness in your life instead of using force and strength all the time.

The constant nagging and feeling of ingratitude in you blocks every opportunity, happiness and sense of enjoyment. No benefit can be enjoyed by you unless you abandon these feelings. With your narrow thinking, you do not understand the meaning of baby steps. You want to gulp down all you have in seconds. Patience, even the word, means nothing to you. Unwillingness to grow out of this narrow-mindedness makes you feel sick. Your immobility in thoughts makes it more evident through your legs thus you feel disabled, metaphorically and literally as well.

Karmic Alignment

You are very well-acquainted with the laws of the universe. Rather than adding more to the problems, your mission on earth is to bring resolve, commitment and love in ways unimaginable. You are the peace-maker but your habit of becoming an instigator harms you in ways countless.

Let go of all the negativity you have in your mind regarding the different cultures, traditions and countries. We all are one. If you despise one out of so many, the day is not far away when you will despise yours too. Instead of being aggressive, always, you must choose the lighter and more flexible way of dealing with matters. Push your limits. Bring everything to a close. You mustn't leave the projects in between, unfinished.

Working good on a global scale helps only when you are thankful for the little things too. Imprint gratitude in your mind, body and soul. Do not be afraid of aiming high, dreaming and thinking of things which seem impossible for you because a day will come when you shall be surprised how the universe changed certain paths to let you meet your destiny.

Keep faith in the abundance of the universe. Start projects on a global scale, finish them unfalteringly. If you align with the universe, no obstacle can beat you down, rather you shall be much more accomplished.

Affirmation

I am a peacemaker. I strive and thrive for the greater good. I believe my abilities.

22

THE FOOL

Introduction

Taking a massive leap of faith in the universe and its magic, this karma also called the beggar is all about starting anew. Being open to what the universe has to offer, this karmic number ensures the potential of the inherent. It is associated with naivety and innocence which the inherent may have as he is unaware of the risks involved in the path that he has chosen for himself.

Logics are overpowered here by the intuitive abilities of the inherent. In fact it also represents the feelings of loyalty and companionship. A fool proof chance of taking the new road than the old beaten path can lead to something miraculous, this karmic alignment number shows potential for opportunities and growth in many ways. However the inherent must let go of the fears, the self-doubts and the worries which weighs him down.

Exploration and globetrotting becomes the way of life for the inherent. However, he must take care of his present in order to enjoy the future too.

Positive Characteristics

Rainbows and unicorns! Everything can be achieved if will-power and determination along with perseverance are joined together. Limitations are for the ones who do not know the rules of the universe-the sole rule is feel the taste of true freedom. In this way, the enlightenment works which is called foolishness in terms of the ones who spiritually unaligned. Anyone who is currently able to exhibit these qualities in their nature must know that they are under the positive manifestation of the 22nd Karmic Alignment number also called the Madman or the beggar.

If you are also perceiving the world as an enlightened soul, you may know that your happiness is contagious. This is how you have been curated by the God. You are so grateful to get an opportunity to be in the human form that you look at even the ugliest thing, if there's any for you, with an amazement of a kid. Isn't that beautiful? You don't have to find a reason to smile because everything in this world makes you happy.

Freedom to you is the motto of life. Nobody can try to cage you. If anybody tries to, you shall drop the luxuries and everything that comes with bondage at a drop of a hat and shall remove the chains and tread your own path but staying a slave? Nah! Not in this birth. Practically speaking, when you choose the less-chosen path, you meet endless difficulties on your way however you are a soul who will perceive every difficulty with a smile and will rock with every easy step, if there's any.

Do you give a flying goose to anybody watching you? No, not even in your wildest dreams. You consider your happiness and freedom much bigger factor to stay happy rather than worrying what others might think of you. Equality sounds good to you whereas biasness is what breaks your patience. You simply move out of the equation.

Your life is like a fireworks display with an enormous drop of detachment. You do not get attached to anyone or anything. Your gift of gab works wonders. You tend to make friends easily.

Nature is your best friend. You can ditch your birthday party in a discotheque for a walk in the nearby woods with your friends. You feel protected because you align with the law of the universe-detached and free. The whole earth is one happy place for you. You do not understand the religions and ethnicities but consider every human equal and same.

Earthly roads, heavenly heights, slick skies-you live for it all. You find it hard to stay at one place for a long time. You like to move around a lot.

Simply saying, your life may not be a bed of roses but your way of living definitely makes it look like a bed of roses.

Negative Characteristics

What a 180 degree turn of events in the life of the inherent. Do you feel that you are stuck in one place? That your home is the prison? Do you feel negligent and unwilling to work? Does your boss call you unreliable? Do you even have any goals?

If the answer is yes to more than 3 questions, then you have entered the negative manifestation of the 22nd karmic number. Darling, it is not you who is stuck but your narrow-mindedness. Change your thinking-process and you shall change the circumstances.

You lose freedom in many ways. Lack of money? Lack of trust? Jealousy? Lack of clarity? Unable to speak out your thoughts? Illnesses? Obsession of showing off for recognition? These are some of the ways you lose your much needed freedom. You may become despotic human with such domineering vices that others may get scared of you and start staying away from you.

Planning for the future is a part of life. You can change jobs but without any security? You are inviting trouble. Impulsive decision-making can also create ruckus in your life.

There are different ways to handle situations but staying away from any sort of relationships is never the solution. You always, always, impose your rules and principles on others whether these are required or not. Refrain from such impositions. These are typical stereotypes.

Grow out of the stereotypes. Become flexible in your approach. Pay gratitude for what you own.

Karmic Alignment

Respect for what people are. Respect yourself. Trust God in aligning your life. Find happiness around you. External factors matter but what matters more is your sense of belief. You are the creator of your own destiny. Own it.

Freedom is your calling, jealousy isn't. Set your targets. Achieve your goals. Dream big. Start small. But what matters the most is your freedom of choice. Attaching yourself to goals may hinder the success however detachment is the key.

Epitomise happiness, epitomise freedom and joy. Set an example for the weak spirits to tap their hidden potential. You must believe in yourself before believing others. Open your heart. Let the sadness go away. Let go of the attachments. Believe in yourself and your abilities.

Travel like loners. Learn the philosophies of the world. Learn to juggle difficult situations. However try to fit in the social norms. You have unconditional love for everyone and everything. Exhibit it. Feel it. Let others feel it too.

Align with the laws of the universe. You may seek freedom but you are already free at heart. Reach the highest level of spirituality.

Affirmation

I am a free soul. My work is to spread love and kindness everywhere. The divinity has bestowed me with enormous potential to make this world a better place to live in.

Epilogue

While comprehending the 22 Karmic Alignment numbers must have been a journey never experienced or heard before, the inquisitiveness about the future never ends. The more one knows, the more one thinks he knows less, isn't that right? The karmic alignment theory has been a ground-shaking and earth-shattering phenomenon owing to which many people have understood the concept of karma theory.

Sri Krishna says in Bhagwad Geeta,

अचोद्यमानानि यथा, पुष्पाणि फलानि च।
स्वं कालं नातिवर्तन्ते, तथा कर्म पुरा कृतम्।

Achodyamanani yatha, puspani falani ch.
Svam kalam nativartante, tatha karm pura krutam.

Even the fruits and flowers wait for none when ripening and blooming respectively, hence the humans must wait for none while performing their karmas to achieve the results thereof.

With total awe, I have decided to abide by this quote by Sri Krishna and hence launch my next book associated with the yearly predictions based on the karmic numerology. Primarily based on how you shall know through the help of the karma theory that whether your karma numbers will make or break your next year, this book will be the blueprint of the successful endeavours of your life.

www.ingramcontent.com/pod-product-compliance
Lightning Source LLC
LaVergne TN
LVHW041930070526
838199LV00051BA/2767